Idea Bags

Activities to Promote the School-to-Home Connection

by
Sharon MacDonald

illustrated by
Corbin Hillam

Published by Fearon Teacher Aids
an imprint of

McGraw-Hill Children's Publishing

Credits

Author: Sharon MacDonald
Cover and Inside Design: Good Neighbor Press, Inc.
Cover and Inside Illustrations: Corbin Hillam
Executive Editor: Kristin Eclov
Editor: Cindy Barden

McGraw-Hill
Children's Publishing

A Division of The McGraw-Hill Companies

Published by Fearon Teacher Aids
An imprint of McGraw-Hill Children's Publishing
Copyright © 1999 McGraw-Hill Children's Publishing

Send all inquiries to:
McGraw-Hill Children's Publishing
3195 Wilson Drive NW
Grand Rapids, Michigan 49544

Idea Bags–grades PreK-1
ISBN: 0-7682-0283-3

3 4 5 6 7 8 9 PHXBK 07 06 05 04 03

Table of Contents

What's an Idea Bag? iv

Parent Letter vi

Idea Bags

Autumn 1

Ants 4

Being Sick 7

Clay 11

Construction 15

Colors 19

The Do-Nothing Machine 22

Eclipse 25

Faces 29

Wiggly, Fuzzy Caterpillar 33

Globe 37

Glue 40

Lemonade 44

My Little Brother 49

My Ears 52

Neighborhood 55

Pulley 58

Scissors 61

Stories on the Road 64

String 67

Tying Shoes 71

The Beach 75

Water 79

Tabletop Blocks 83

Community Workers 87

Frog 92

Painting 96

What Can I Do? 100

You and Me 104

What's an Idea Bag?

Fun Ideas to Share with Children

Ants

If I were a little black ant
I know what I would say
To all of my ant buddies
Who work so hard all day.

"Stop!" I'd shout in ant-talk.
"Let's rest upon this leaf,
Or swing upon this spider's web
He won't mind if we're brief."

I know the ants would tell me
The secret of their strength,
How they move those boulders,
And trees three times their length.

Down their hole I'd slide
Into their hidden spaces.
We'd talk and eat and crawl around,
Exploring strange new places.

Then home with me they'd come
And play with all my toys.
We'd colonize my room.
We wouldn't make much noise.

I think the ants would want to,
But I couldn't really say,
'Cause they might not like the smell
The bug man sprayed today!

An Idea Bag is a brown paper lunch bag filled with ideas parents can use at home to help further their children's learning. Idea Bags invite parents to do activities with their children to reinforce and expand concepts taught at school. The suggestions aim to capture parents' interest and involve them with their children's education in a non-threatening way. Idea Bags allow parents to learn first, then teach their children.

Each Idea Bag focuses on a single topic. The poem attached to the front of the lunch bag sets the topic, and the activities provided inside relate to it. Idea Bags deal with more than the surface of a topic. Often, there is considerable depth in a particular set of activities. Parents can expand their children's knowledge of subjects by completing the activities with their children. Most of the activities can be done with materials found around the house or from recycled consumer products.

The activities range in difficulty, so a broad cross-section of children with different skill levels and abilities can participate. Skills and concepts taught include math, arts and crafts, language arts, listening and writing skills, dance and movement, hands-on science, creative thinking, and social studies.

Idea Bags can be sent home every other week with students during the school year, and seasonal topics can be sent at the appropriate time of the year. For example, the "Autumn" Idea Bag can be sent home in September or early October.

How to Make an Idea Bag

To make an Idea Bag, photocopy the poem, trim it to fit, and attach it to the outside of a brown paper lunch bag with tape, glue, or a stapler. Photocopy the activities for that poem. Fold the sheets in the middle and slide them into the bag. If possible, make two-sided copies to save paper. Parent volunteers or students from an upper grade could do the photocopying and make up the Idea Bags in advance. If parents offer to donate supplies, suggest a package of 50 or 100 lunch bags.

While Idea Bags are excellent tools for involving parents, they easily fit into classroom use as well. If you're are talking about communities in class, you might read the poem "Neighborhood" (page 55) or "Community Workers" (page 87) to the children. If you decide not to send the Idea Bags home, you can use many of the suggestions in class.

When Idea Bags are sent home for the first time, include an introductory letter to the parents. This provides a brief explanation of Idea Bags and defines expectations. You are welcome to copy the parent letter on the next page, and change or rewrite it to suit your individual needs.

The activities in the Idea Bags are NOT homework. Nothing needs to be returned to school. The activities constitute "constructive play" that result in learning. It is not important that all activities be done, only that parents and children spend time together.

Idea Bags are not a cure-all for getting parents involved. Some parents will use them, while others will not for a variety of reasons. Parents' time, priorities, energy, and attention are limited. As teachers, we can provide resources and encourage parents to use them.

Idea Bags offer a way for teachers to send home fun projects that are different from what parents usually receive from school. Many parents will find the Idea Bags interesting, helpful, and fun to use with their children.

You will probably not be able to get all parents involved, but some will, and that makes it worth the effort. Do your best to reach as many as you can. That is what Idea Bags are all about.

Dear Parent(s):

Many of you have asked for ideas to do at home to help with your child's education. Today your child has brought home an Idea Bag. You will find a poem on the front of the bag and many ideas on the activity sheets inside. Select one or all of the activities to enjoy with your child.

The activities range in difficulty, so children with different skill levels and abilities can participate. Skills and concepts taught include math, arts and crafts, language arts, listening and writing skills, dance and movement, hands-on science, creative thinking, and social studies. Many activities are designed to help young children improve hand-eye coordination and motor skills as they have fun.

This is NOT homework. Idea Bags are a resource of fun activities to do with your child. If your schedule is too busy this week, save the activities for the weekend or next week. Involve others, like your baby-sitter, grandparents, or other friends or relatives who would enjoy completing some of the activities with your child.

Many of the activities can be done with several children of different ages, so include other family members whenever possible. Invite your child's friends or same-age relatives to join in the fun. The more the merrier.

Most of the materials needed for the activities are items available around the house. Some will need to be purchased. If you have difficulty finding materials for a particular activity, please let me know. We can help track down the items you need.

Idea Bags will be sent home about every two weeks. Enjoy completing the activities and spending quality time with your child. Your comments, ideas, and suggestions about the Idea Bags are welcome.

Sincerely,

Autumn

As autumn leaves
fall all around,
They make a blanket
on the ground.
When winter winds
begin to blow,
The roots are safe
from the freezing snow.

Cut along dashed line and glue to a brown paper lunch bag.

1

Make Friends with a Tree

You will need:

    Stethoscope (Stethoscopes can be purchased at a medical supply house for about $5.)

    Magnifying glass

    Crayons

    Paper

Take children outside to "meet" a tree. Introduce the tree as though it were another person. (Jill, I'd like you to meet Mr. Elm Tree. Mr. Elm Tree, this is Jill.)

Let children listen to the tree with a stethoscope. Have them examine the bark and leaves with a magnifying glass. To make tree-bark rubbings, remove the wrapper from a crayon. Have children place a sheet of paper on the tree and rub back and forth with the side of the crayon. If possible, take photographs of the children with the tree during the different seasons of the year.

Tell children that there is one really great thing about having a tree for a friend. If you tell the tree a secret, it will never tell your secret to anyone else.

Rake and Jump

Most children love to jump into piles of leaves, so let them help rake the leaves into large piles. Show them what happens when the leaves are tossed in the wind. Invite other children from the neighborhood to join the rake-and-jump party. When everyone is tired, make hot cocoa for all to enjoy.

Fun Ideas to Share with Children

On the outside of this bag you will find the poem *Autumn*. Read the poem aloud with children.

Explain that autumn is another word for fall. Fall is one of the four seasons. Ask children if they can name the other three seasons.

Leaf Sort and Match

Go on a fall walk with children. As you discover different kinds of leaves, collect a few of each kind. Encourage children to use their senses to observe the many fall colors, to smell the leaves, to feel the texture of the leaves, and to listen to the delightful crunching sound when they walk through dry leaves.

After your walk have children sort leaves by size, by shape, and by color. Talk about how the leaves are the same and how they are different. Encourage children to examine leaves with a magnifying glass.

Leaf Rubbings

You will need:

    Red, yellow, gold, orange, and brown crayons

    White paper

    Leaves

    Glue or glue stick

    Cardboard

Peel the wrappers off the crayons. Have children glue leaves to cardboard and place white paper over the leaves. Using the side of a crayon, have them rub back and forth across the paper over the leaves. The leaf image will be transferred to the paper.

Preserve Fall Leaves

You will need:

    Leaves
    Waxed paper
    Iron and ironing board
    Cardboard
    Glue, glue stick, or tape
    White paper
    Clear plastic page protectors

Help children collect leaves with lots of red, orange, gold, and yellow colors. Heat an iron to medium (no steam). Place waxed paper on a piece of cardboard on the ironing board. Place leaves carefully on the waxed paper, then cover them with another sheet of waxed paper and a sheet of plain paper. Carefully iron over the top paper. This heats the waxed paper, which places wax on one side of the leaves. Carefully turn the waxed paper and leaves over and iron the other side. Ironing coats the leaves with wax, keeping them colorful and intact for a long time. Adult supervision is necessary for this activity.

Children can glue or tape the leaves to paper and keep them in clear plastic page protectors or "magnetic" pages from a photo album.

The Giving Tree

Get a copy of *The Giving Tree* by Shel Silverstein (Harper & Row, 1964) from your library and read it out loud to children. Talk about all the ways the tree is useful to the boy. Ask how trees are useful to them, to birds and animals, and to people in general.

Leaf Collage

Collect fall leaves in the Idea Bag that children brought home. Let children make a fall collage by gluing the leaves to the outside of the bag.

The Changing Seasons

You will need:

    Large sheet of paper
    Crayons or markers

Fold the paper to divide it into four equal sections. Draw a tree with no leaves in one section. Copy the same drawing to the other three sections. Label the sections *Spring, Summer, Winter,* and *Fall.* Write lightly in pencil.

Have children trace over the letters with crayons or markers, then complete the trees by drawing leaves for each season. They can add other details to the drawings, like a snowman by the winter tree, blossoms on the spring tree, a bird in the summer tree, and apples on the fall tree.

3-D Fall Tree

You will need:

    Coffee can
    Several small rocks
    Construction paper in fall colors
    Scissors
    Crayons or markers
    Tape
    Acorns, pinecones, and other fall nuts and seeds
      (optional)

Place the branch in a coffee can. Secure it by placing several small rocks in the can around the bottom of the branch.

Let children cut leaf shapes from colored construction paper.

Have children use tape to attach the fall leaves to the branches of their "tree." They can tape or tie acorns, pinecones, and other fall nuts and seeds to the tree if these are available.

Ants

If I were a little black ant
I know what I would say
To all of my ant buddies
Who work so hard all day.

"Stop!" I'd shout in ant-talk.
"Let's rest upon this leaf;
Or swing upon this spider's web
He won't mind if we're brief."

I know the ants would tell me
The secret of their strength,
How they move those boulders,
And trees three times their length.

Down their hole I'd slide
Into their hidden spaces.
We'd talk and eat and crawl around,
Exploring strange new places.

Then home with me they'd come
And play with all my toys.
We'd colonize my room.
We wouldn't make much noise.

I think the ants would want to,
But I couldn't really say,
'Cause they might not like the smell.
The bug man sprayed today!

Cut along dashed line and glue to a brown paper lunch bag.

Ant Mounds

You will need:

- Plastic ants (They can be bought at a store where party supplies are sold.)
- Plastic dishpan
- Sand

Fill a dishpan one-quarter full of damp sand. Let children make ant mounds and place the plastic ants on the mounds. Have children form the holes in the top of the mounds and show the ants coming and going.

Use the ants for counting activities and simple addition and subtraction story problems. For example: *Two ants are going into the ant mound. Two ants are coming out of the ant mound. How many ants are there in all?*

Paint Black Ants

You will need:

- Washable black paint
- Cotton swab
- Plastic container
- White paper

Pour a small amount of washable black paint in a container. Have children dip the cotton swab in the paint and make ants all over the paper.

Fun Ideas to Share with Children

On the outside of this bag you will find the poem *Ants*. Read the poem aloud with children.

Talk about ants with children. Discuss what they look like, how many legs and antennae they have, and where they live.

If You Were an Ant

Ask children, "If you were an ant, what would you like to do?" Have them draw action pictures of themselves as ants.

Ant Puzzles

You will need:

- A picture of ants around an anthill (This could be photocopied from a reference book or download one from the Internet.)
- Scissors
- Cardboard
- Glue or glue stick
- Envelope or resealable sandwich bag

Glue the picture to cardboard. Cut the picture into as many puzzle pieces as children can manage. After children make the puzzle, place the pieces in an envelope or resealable bag for use another time.

March and Sing

You will need:

- The words to the song "The Ants Go Marching" (If you don't know the words, ask an older child or check with your local library.)

March and sing the song with children on your nature walks.

Ants-on-a-Log Snack

You will need:

    Celery

    Raisins

    Butter knife

    Paper towel

    Peanut butter or soft cream cheese

Wash and cut celery into three-inch (7.5-cm) sticks. Dry the celery with a paper towel. Have children spread peanut butter or soft cream cheese on the celery (the log) and place raisins (the ants) in the peanut butter. Children love eating ants on a log.

Clay Ants and Ant Mounds

You will need:

    1 cup flour

    1/2 cup salt

    2 tablespoons cream of tartar

    1 tablespoon vegetable oil

    1 cup water

    3 or 4 drops of food coloring

To make your own modeling clay, mix ingredients well. Have an adult pour the mixture into an electric skillet and cook at 350 degrees until the dough pulls away from the sides of the skillet and can easily be formed into a ball. Scrape it onto a board and knead well.

When it cools, let children make their own clay ants and ant mounds. Working on an old plastic placemat, shower curtain liner, or tablecloth keeps clay from sticking to the table. After use, store clay in an airtight container. It will last four to six weeks.

Note: Food coloring can be difficult to remove from clothing and other surfaces. Be sure children wear old "paint clothes," and work areas are covered whenever food coloring is used in an activity.

Estimate How Many Ants

Go for a nature walk in your neighborhood. Find an ant mound. Ask children to estimate how many ants live in the mound.

Ask children, "Could all the ants be counted one by one?" "Would that be hard to do?" "Why?"

Explain that sometimes we must estimate the number of ants, people, plants, and other items, since it would be impossible to count each one individually.

Make Predictions

This activity helps children understand the scientific approach to learning: asking questions, making predictions, running experiments, and observing results.

You will need:

    3 peas

    3 small pieces of bread

    3 small pieces of cookie

Take the food items to an ant mound. Ask children, "Which food do you think the ants will eat first?" Have children make a prediction about the ants' favorite food. Leave the food on the ant mound. Return to the mound daily and observe.

More About Ants

You and the children can learn more about ants by checking out nonfiction books from the public library. For a simplified explanation of the ant world, try *Ant Cities* by Arthur Dorros (HarperCollins). Two fiction books about ants that children might enjoy are *Lucky Me* by Denys Cazet (Orchard Books) and *Two Bad Ants* by Chris Van Allsburg (Houghton Mifflin).

Being Sick

Being sick is *yucky!*

I ache from toe to head.

I take some awful medicine,

And spend long days in bed.

Being sick is such a bore,

There is nothing much to do.

I watch TV, or play with toys,

Or read about "Winnie-the-Pooh."

Being sick is not much fun!

But when I do recover,

I feel so smart and smug because,

I gave it to my brother!

Cut along dashed line and glue to a brown paper lunch bag.

7

Fun Ideas to Share with Children

Look at X-rays

You will need:

X-rays from family members

Place X-rays in a window on a sunny day so children can see them clearly. Talk about what doctors look for when they look at X-rays and how people look inside their skin. Emphasize how important it is to take care of your body, inside as well as outside.

The Doctor's Office

Call your doctor's office to set up a time for children to visit with the doctor. Do it when children are well so they can look around and explore without worrying about shots or an exam. A pre-visit allows children to become familiar with the office and surroundings, and meet the doctor in a pleasant environment. Children will be less fearful when the need arises for a real visit. Ask the nurse to show children a few of the instruments the doctor uses, and explain how they work and what they are used for (a stethoscope, tongue depressor, thermometer, and blood pressure cuff are good choices).

On the outside of this bag you will find the poem *Being Sick*. Read the poem aloud with children.

Talk about how germs are spread. Explain why it is important to keep people and animals healthy.

A Stay-Healthy Book

You will need:

3 to 5 sheets of white paper
Construction paper, 1 sheet
Stapler
Crayons, markers, or colored pencils
Old magazines
Blunt scissors
Glue, glue stick, or tape

Fold the sheets of white paper and the construction paper in half. Staple the pages together in the center with the construction paper on the outside for the cover of the book.

Have children draw pictures in their books, showing ways to stay healthy. Help children find pictures in old magazines of children sleeping, eating, going to the doctor, exercising, and dressing properly for cold weather. Children can cut out the pictures and glue or tape them in their books.

Ask children to dictate stories to match the pictures. Write their stories in their books. Read the stories back to children at a later date.

An X-Ray Machine

You will need:

  Sharp knife
  Crayons or markers
  Scissors
  Paper
  Large cardboard box, like one used to
    pack a television

Cut a hole in the bottom of the box large enough so children can crawl in through the top, stand up, and stick their heads out through the hole. Have children draw their pretend bones on a blank side of the box with crayons or markers. If the box doesn't have a blank side, cover one side with butcher paper.

Glue paper circles on the front for knobs to turn the X-ray machine on and off. Children can write "X-ray machine" on the box.

Play Doctor

You will need:

  Dolls, action figures, or stuffed animals
  Pretend medical instruments
    (You can buy them or make your own.)
  Adhesive bandages

Encourage children to play doctor with dolls, action figures, or stuffed toys. Give them pretend medical instruments and encourage them to talk about the fears their dolls and stuffed animals have when they go to the doctor.

Children love adhesive bandages, so give them several to use on dolls or themselves. Adhesive bandages make everything better!

The Sick-Day Box

Let children help make a sick-day box to use when they are sick. Go through favorite books, toys, coloring books, stuffed animals, and games with the children. Let them help choose a few items to place in the sick-day box. Include crayons, markers, stickers, yarn, a glue stick, scraps of material or wallpaper, puzzles, and blank paper. Talk about the purpose of the box—to keep special items for use only when they are sick.

Use a Stethoscope

You will need:

   Stethoscope (Stethoscopes can be purchased
      at a medical supply house for about $5.)
   Chalk or washable marker
   Small paper heart

Trace a silhouette of a child on a full-length mirror
with chalk or washable marker. Tape a paper heart
on the silhouette in the approximate place of the
heart. Let children stand in front of the silhouette
and use the stethoscope to listen to their hearts.

Stethoscopes are great for young children to use
under supervision. They will listen to everything!

Body Puzzle

You will need:

   Large sheet of paper (butcher paper
      works well)
   Pencil
   Blunt scissors
   Crayons, markers, or colored pencils
   Resealable sandwich bag

Trace around children's
bodies on large sheets
of paper. Have them
color the shapes and cut
them out. Cut the body
shapes into as many
puzzle pieces as you
think children can
assemble without losing
interest. After making the
puzzle, store pieces in a
resealable sandwich
bag. Children will work
the puzzle over and
over again.

Jumpin' Germs

Talk about how germs travel from place to place.
Some travel through the air on coughs and sneezes.
Germs can move from one person's hands to
another's hands. Talk about how unwashed hands
spread germs and how soap kills germs that cause
sickness.

Have children
demonstrate how
they wash their hands
to kill germs, especially
before eating. Remind
them to wash "both"
sides of their hands.

Lead children in a
discussion about how
coughing and sneezing
spread germs. Talk
about how using a tissue and covering their
mouths when coughing or sneezing help reduce the
spread of germs through the air.

Body Math

Help children practice counting fingers and toes.
Count to ten. Count backwards from ten to one.
Use fingers and toes to count to twenty and back
again.

Do simple addition by holding up several fingers on
one hand and having children count them, then hold
up several fingers on the other hand. Ask them how
many fingers you are holding up altogether.

Do simple subtraction by holding up fingers on one
or both hands. Have children count the number of
fingers. Close two or three fingers and ask
children how many are left.

Clay

What's hiding in my clay today
Waiting to come out?
I hope it's something wonderful.
A dinosaur?
No doubt.

I pushed on it, I pulled on it,
I punched it in the middle.
It ooched between my fingers,
But it only changed a little.

I worked a very long, long time
To see what I could make.
But only two things worked out right:
A lumpy pancake and a snake.

Both my eyes said, "Dinosaur!"
But my hands could not obey.
I know they're just not ready
To make what I see from clay.

Someday I will get better
If I keep working with my clay.
I'll find that dinosaur sometime,
Tomorrow or some other day.

Cut along dashed line and glue to a brown paper lunch bag.

11

Fun Ideas to Share with Children

Cooked Play-Clay

You will need:

- 1 cup flour
- 1/2 cup salt
- 2 tablespoons cream of tartar
- 1 tablespoon vegetable oil
- 1 cup water
- 3 or 4 drops of food coloring
- Cookie cutters

Mix ingredients well. Have an adult pour the mixture into an electric skillet and cook at 350 degrees until the dough pulls away from the sides of the skillet and can easily be formed into a ball. Scrape it onto a board and knead well.

Cover the work surface. When it cools, let children flatten the clay and use cookie cutters to make shapes. Children can pound, push, roll, and cut the clay into lots of shapes and designs. After use, store clay in an airtight container. It will last four to six weeks. Remind children NOT to eat the clay.

Note: Food coloring can be difficult to remove from clothing and other surfaces. Be sure children wear old "paint clothes," and work areas are covered whenever food coloring is used in an activity.

On the outside of this bag you will find the poem *Clay*. Read the poem aloud with children.

Children enjoy experimenting with clay. Several ideas for making and using different types and textures of clay are included. Allowing children to participate in making clay will add to the fun. When working with clay, cover the work surface with an old plastic placemat, shower curtain liner, or tablecloth to prevent the clay from sticking to your table.

Potter's Clay

You will need:

- Potter's clay (available at craft stores)
- Small bowl of water
- Cookie sheet or other type of tray

Cover work surface. Give each child a large ball of potter's clay. Have children wet their hands before working the clay. This makes the clay easier to mold into shape. Let children make shapes from the clay. Remind them NOT to eat the clay. Store clay in a tightly sealed container between uses.

Uncooked Play-Clay

You will need:
- 1 cup flour
- 1/3 cup salt
- 1/3 cup water
- 3 or 4 drops of food coloring
- Craft sticks

Blend the ingredients thoroughly, kneading the dough well. Cover the work area. Let children make balls of play-clay and flatten it to make pretend pizzas. They can cut the pizzas with craft sticks and have a pretend pizza party. After use, store clay in an airtight container. It will last about two weeks. Remind children NOT to eat the clay.

Grainy-Textured Clay

You will need:
- 1 cup sand
- 1/2 cup cornstarch
- 1 teaspoon alum
- 3/4 cup hot water

Have an adult mix sand, cornstarch, and alum in a pan. Add hot water and stir vigorously. Cook mixture over medium heat until it thickens. Let it cool.

Cover the work area. After children make their clay sculptures, set them outside in the sunlight for a day or two to dry. They will dry to a stone-like finish. Store unused clay in an airtight container. Remind children NOT to eat the clay.

A Unique Sensory Experience

You will need:
- 1 cup powdered laundry detergent
- 1/8 cup water

Beat the detergent and water together vigorously with a heavy spoon or eggbeater. Cover the work area. This clay can be molded into almost any form. Suggest that children make duck or boat shapes. The clay hardens when it dries—making soap for the bathtub that may provide an additional incentive to bathe! Remind children NOT to eat the clay.

Cornstarch Clay

You will need:
- 1 cup salt
- 1/3 cup cornstarch
- 1/3 cup water

Heat the water slowly, adding cornstarch and salt. Stir until well mixed. Knead the dough. Add water, a few drops at a time, if clay is too dry. This type of clay has a more gritty texture than ordinary clay.

Cover the work surface. Have children work the clay into animal and people shapes. The clay will dry without cracking. Remind children NOT to eat the clay.

Sawdust Clay Smells Terrific

You will need:

1 1/2 tablespoons flour
1 cup water
1/4 teaspoon salt
2 cups sawdust

Make a paste by mixing the flour and water. Have an adult cook it over medium heat until it's thick and heavy, like cream. Add salt. Let children use their hands to mix the paste with two cups of sawdust until the sawdust and paste form a ball. If it is too sticky, add more sawdust. If it is too dry, add a few drops of water.

Sawdust clay dries hard, but it is light in weight and very durable. Store unused clay it in an airtight container. Remind children NOT to eat the clay.

Edible Pretzel Clay

You will need:

1 package dry yeast
1 1/2 cup warm water
1 teaspoon salt
1 tablespoon sugar
4 cups flour
1 egg (beaten)
Salt (optional, for taste)

Pour the warm water into a bowl and sprinkle in the yeast. Stir until well mixed. Add salt, sugar, and flour. Have children mix the ingredients well and knead the dough. Children can roll and twist the clay into pretzel shapes.

Place the pretzel creations on a greased cookie sheet. Brush the pretzels with beaten egg. Sprinkle with salt to taste. Bake for 12 to 15 minutes at 350 degrees or until golden brown. Eat when cool. This is SPECIAL clay that can be eaten. Ordinary clay should NOT be eaten.

Peanut-Butter Clay

You will need:

1/2 cup peanut butter
1/2 cup non-fat powdered milk
2/3 cup honey

Blend ingredients in a bowl and knead until it reaches a dough-like consistency. Have children wash hands thoroughly before they pound, poke, shape, and cut the clay. Suggest they make peanut butter cookie shapes. Criss-cross the tops of the cookies with a plastic fork. When they finish playing, children can eat their creations. Remind them that this is SPECIAL clay that can be eaten and that ordinary clay should NOT be eaten.

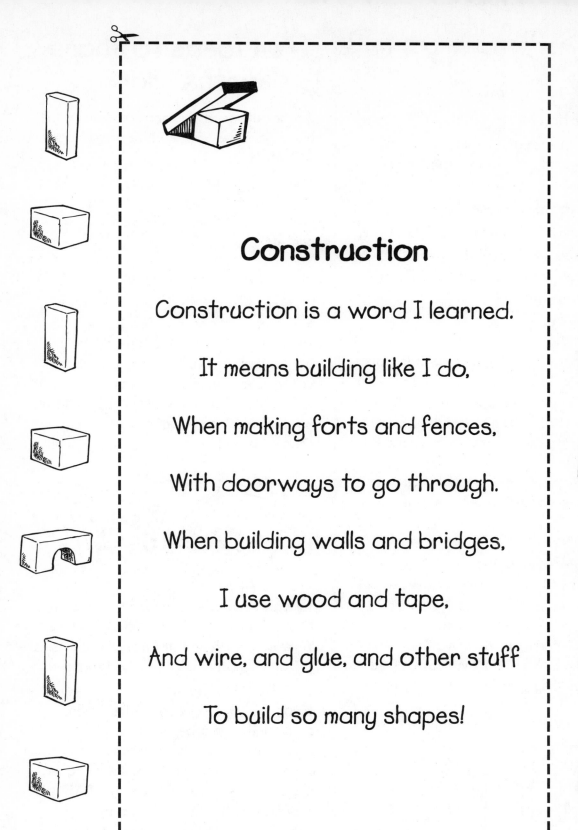

Construction

Construction is a word I learned.

It means building like I do,

When making forts and fences,

With doorways to go through.

When building walls and bridges,

I use wood and tape,

And wire, and glue, and other stuff

To build so many shapes!

Cut along dashed line and glue to a brown paper lunch bag.

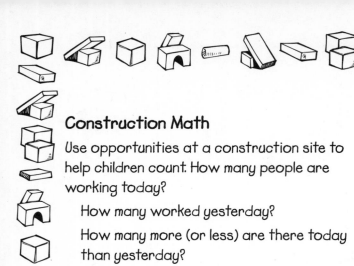

Construction Math

Use opportunities at a construction site to help children count. How many people are working today?

How many worked yesterday?

How many more (or less) are there today than yesterday?

How many windows are in the building?

How many doors?

How many floors?

Wood-Scrap and Glue Constructions

You will need:

Wood scraps in various sizes and shapes (These can usually be obtained free from a job site or at a lumberyard, if you ask.)

Non-toxic, water soluble wood glue

Buttons, scraps of material, string, yarn, etc.

Newspaper

Sand rough edges to avoid slivers. Cover work area with newspaper. Let children build with wood scraps, gluing pieces together. They can add decorations by gluing on buttons, scraps of material, bottle caps, string, or yarn. Let them have a free hand unless they specifically ask for help.

Fun Ideas to Share with Children

On the outside of this bag you will find the poem *Construction*. Read the poem aloud with children.

Young children are fascinated with building tall towers and playing with building materials like boxes, blocks, and plastic buckets.

Visit a Construction Site

Visit a nearby construction site frequently. Ask children to observe changes since their last visit. Point out that different workers are needed at different times during the building process to lay the foundation, build walls, put in plumbing and electrical fixtures, do finish work, paint, put in sidewalks and driveways, and so on.

Take along a camera or pencil and paper. Photograph or sketch the building site as it looks on your first visit. On each successive visit, take another photo or add changes to your drawing.

If you took photographs, children can arrange them in order to show the progress of the building. Let them tape each photo to a separate sheet of paper and write a sentence or two to tell what is happening in the picture or what has changed since the last picture. Staple the pages together to make a book.

Build with Boxes

You will need:

> Empty boxes in a variety of shapes and sizes
> Newspaper
> White glue or tape
> Decorative scraps

Cover work area with newspaper. Let children make structures by gluing or taping boxes together. Provide decorative scraps for attaching to the structures with glue or tape.

Styrofoam Poke-Along

You will need:

> Styrofoam™ pieces from the "Build with Styrofoam™" activity
> Toothpicks, straws, screws, paper clips, small twigs, craft sticks, or other objects that can be poked into Styrofoam™

Let children poke objects into Styrofoam™ blocks to construct buildings, animals, people, or imaginary critters. You never know what will result from scrap materials and imagination!

Build with Styrofoam™

You will need:

> Styrofoam™
> Craft knife or handsaw
> 2" to 3" (5-cm to 7.5-cm) strips of self-adhesive Velcro™

Have an adult cut large pieces of Styrofoam™ into smaller rectangles and squares with a craft knife or handsaw. (Cutting Styrofoam™ can be messy. Do it outside, if possible.) Attach Velcro™ strips to several sides of each Styrofoam™ shape.

Let children put the Styrofoam™ pieces together randomly by sticking Velcro™ sides together to make structures. Encourage children to try different combinations and shapes.

What's in a Box of Paper Clips?

You will need:

> Box of paper clips (The larger-size ones or those coated with colored plastic work well.)

To begin, have children make long chains of paper clips. Then let children create shapes and constructions by hooking the clips at various points along the chain. If you thought paper clips were only for holding paper together, you may be pleasantly surprised at what comes out of a box of paper clips! A box of paper clips can entertain children for hours. This is also a good way to help children pass time during a long car trip.

Build with PVC Pipe

You will need:

Short pieces of PVC pipe

Pipe connectors

PVC pipe and connectors offer great opportunities for children to build. Let children put the pipe and connectors together in a variety of ways. Take the PVC structures outside on a sunny day and run water through them. See if there are any leaks!

Thread Spool Constructions

You will need:

Empty thread spools

(These can be obtained from dressmakers or stores that do alterations.)

Non-toxic, water soluble wood glue

Newspaper

Buttons

Cover work area with newspaper. Let children stack, glue, and attach spools with wood glue. They can decorate structures by gluing buttons in place.

Twig Sculptures

You will need:

Clean Styrofoam™ trays, like the ones used to package bakery goods

Twigs

String or yarn

Glue

Go for a walk with children and collect twigs. Let children poke the twigs into the Styrofoam™ trays in any pattern they like. The twigs stand up and make interesting designs. Children can connect the twigs with string or yarn. If needed for stability, use glue to fasten the twig bases to the trays to keep them from leaning or falling over.

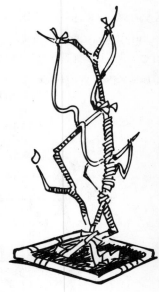

Wet Sand Tracks

You will need:

Toy cars

Dishpan

Wet sand

Cover the bottom of the dishpan with wet sand. Let children roll cars around the dishpan, leaving tracks in the wet sand. Encourage them to talk about the designs they make. Smooth out the tracks in the sand and let children make other designs in the wet sand with toy cars or other objects, like twigs, leaves, craft sticks, pipe cleaners, a sponge, and so on.

Colors

Oh, I wish I had a little red jug to put my colors in.

I'd take them out, go scribble, scribble, scribble,

And put them back again.

Oh, I wish I had a little purple car to put my colors in.

I'd take them out and draw a line,

And put them back again.

Oh, I wish I had a little yellow sun to put my colors in.

I'd take them out, draw round and round,

And put them back again.

Oh, I wish I had a little blue cloud to put my colors in.

I'd take them out, go dot, dot, dot,

And put them back again.

Oh, I wish I had a little orange ball to put my colors in.

I'd take them out, go bounce, bounce, bounce,

And put them back again.

Oh, I've got myself a little green box to put my colors in.

I'll take them out and count them all,

And put them back again.

Note: This poem can be sung to the tune "Polly Wolly Doodle."

Cut along dashed line and glue to a brown paper lunch bag.

Reproducible

Match Colors

You will need:
- Box of 8, 16, or 24 crayons
- Paper

Make a blob of color with each of the crayons on paper. Give children the box of crayons and ask them to match each crayon to its correct color blob. To check if they are correct, children can make their own color blobs next to the original ones to see if they match.

Coloring on Different Surfaces

You will need:
- Crayons
- Plain paper, sandpaper, a brown grocery bag, newspaper, and other colors and textures of paper

Let children use the same color crayon to draw on different types of paper. Have them compare how the same color looks when used on different textures and background colors.

Fun Ideas to Share with Children

On the outside of this bag you will find the poem *Colors*. As you read or sing the poem out loud, have children demonstrate each described movement using the correct color crayon.

Crayon Sort

Give children a box of 16 crayons. Have them sort crayons into three piles: one pile for the darkest colors, one pile for the lightest colors, and one pile for medium shades. This activity helps children practice noticing similarities and differences.

Measure and Draw Lines with a Ruler

You will need:
- Box of 16 crayons
- Ruler
- Paper

Ask children to draw a six-inch (15-cm) red line, a two-inch (5-cm) yellow line, and an eight-inch (20-cm) blue line. Then let children select their own colors and linelengths as they continue to draw lines of various lengths using the ruler. Let lines run into each other, crossing and making designs. When all the lines have been drawn, have children talk about their designs.

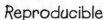

Rub Crayons on Sandpaper
You will need:
    Crayons
    White paper
    Sandpaper
    Coin

Let children color with crayons on sandpaper. Have them try to cover the sandpaper with color. Place the sandpaper in the sun on a hot day, colored side up. After an hour or so, have children place a white sheet of paper over the sandpaper and use a coin to rub gently back and forth across the white paper.

The crayon on the sandpaper will have melted somewhat in the hot sun, allowing the sheet of paper to easily pick up the color from the sandpaper when rubbed. Point out and explain to children the unique color transfer that took place.

Shades of Blue
You will need:
    Box of 64 crayons

Set aside all shades of blue, all shades of red, and all shades of green crayons. Have children put the blue crayons in order by shade from lightest to darkest, then do the same with the red and green crayons.

Measure with Crayons
You will need:
    Stick, string, pencil, book, shoe, and other small objects children can measure
    Crayons
    Tape measure or ruler
    Paper

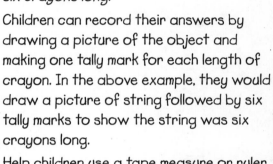

Ask children to use crayons to measure the length of objects. For example: *The string is six crayons long.*

Children can record their answers by drawing a picture of the object and making one tally mark for each length of crayon. In the above example, they would draw a picture of string followed by six tally marks to show the string was six crayons long.

Help children use a tape measure or ruler to measure the same objects. Compare the lengths in crayons to measurements in inches or centimeters.

Write a Crayon Story

Check out the book *Harold and the Purple Crayon* by Crockett Johnson (HarperCollins) from the library. Have children make up similar stories of their own, like "Betty and the Blue Crayon" or "Wendy and the White Crayon." Children can draw pictures and write their own stories.

Children often use invented spelling at this age. At this point, it is more important for them to know they are successful writers than it is for them to spell words correctly.

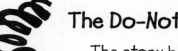

The Do-Nothing Machine

The story begins without
Blueprints or plans.
A rhyming account
Of a child's two hands.

It's the story of John,
The inventor of things,
Who made a machine
From wood, nails, and strings.

He marked his machine
With letters galore.
He couldn't write words.
(He was only four.)

With all kinds of tools,
John spent long hours,
Reworking, remaking,
And adding tall towers.

When friends asked John,
"What does it do?"
"Nothing yet," he'd say.
"I'm not quite through."

The "Do-Nothing Machine"
John named it one day
After months of adding
And taking away.

The fun was in building,
Not what it would do.
John found that out,
And you can too.

So gather together
The best you can find.
Make a "Do-Nothing Machine"
From ideas in your mind.

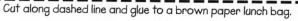
Cut along dashed line and glue to a brown paper lunch bag.

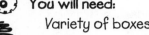

Constructing Machines from Boxes

You will need:

> Variety of boxes, smaller than a shoe box
> Glue
> Jar lids; buttons; scraps of cloth, foil, string, yarn, and wood; thread spools; and other items to attach to boxes
> Markers, crayons, or paints and paintbrush

Let children glue boxes together to make a new kind of machine. When they are finished, they can decorate it by gluing on scraps of whatever you have available. Ask children to name their machines and tell what they do.

Machine Repair Shop

You will need:

> Broken small appliances with the electrical cord cut off (like a toaster, iron, can opener, coffee pot, radio, etc.)
> Assortment of small hand tools (screwdrivers, pliers, tack hammer, adjustable wrench, etc.)
> Wire, string, screws, bolts, nuts, and washers

Loosen the screws and bolts in the appliances so children can take them apart. Let children "repair" the appliances. Supervise this activity closely in case there are any sharp edges that can cause cuts.

Fun Ideas to Share with Children

On the outside of this bag you will find the poem *The Do-Nothing Machine*. Read the poem aloud with children.

This poem gives you an opportunity to talk with children about the many types of machines that we use in our daily lives, from the very simple to the very complex.

Machine Book

You will need:

> Old magazines and ads
> Blunt scissors
> Three-ring binder
> Three-hole-punched paper
> Glue or glue stick
> Pencil or pen

Let children look through old magazines and ads to find and cut out pictures of machines. They can glue the pictures to paper that has been three-hole-punched. They can also draw their own pictures of real or imaginary machines.

Have children tell you what each machine does to help people. Write that below the pictures. Place all the pictures in a three-ring binder to make a "Machine Book." Have children write or dictate stories about the machines in the book.

Imagine Being a Wind-Up Machine

Ask children to think of a machine they would like to be and keep it a secret. Pretend to wind up children, one at a time, with an imaginary key. Have the children dramatize what happens when the machine moves. Guess what machine each child is pretending to be. Let children take turns. You can pretend to be a machine too.

Reproducible

Peanut-Butter Machine

You will need:

  1 cup shelled peanuts
  2 tablespoons vegetable oil
  1/4 teaspoon salt
  Blender
  Bread, muffins, or toast
  Bread knife

If you have a blender, you have a peanut-butter making machine! Let children help shell roasted peanuts. They will probably eat a few, so be sure to have extra. Pour ingredients into the blender. Grind well. Spread on toast, muffins, or bread and enjoy!

Hammer and Nails

You will need:

  Block of soft wood or Styrofoam™
  Long nails with large heads
  Empty thread spools
  Small hammer
    (It's best for young children to use a tack or ball-peen hammer, not a claw hammer.)

Let children place thread spools on blocks of wood or Styrofoam™. They can put nails through the holes in the thread spools and pound them in with a hammer. You may need to help children get the nail started. They can keep pounding until the nail is flush with the top of the thread spool. Using a hammer makes young children feel so grown up! They can add several spools in a row to make knobs for an imaginary remote control.

Caution: This activity needs to be closely supervised.

Take a Machine Walk

Take a walk around the house or through the neighborhood. Help children identify as many machines as they can find. Have them suggest ways each machine helps make our lives easier.

Ask them questions about the machines:

  How do people use them?

  What do they do with them?

  Is it difficult to learn to use that machine?

  Are all machines electrical? What about cars?

  Do all machines have motors? What about a hammer?

Water Painting with a Paintbrush

You will need:

  3" or 4" (7.5-cm or 10-cm) bristle paintbrush
  Bucket of water

Let children "paint" a fence or sidewalk using a brush and bucket of water. When they finish, talk about how a paintbrush is a machine that makes painting easier. Demonstrate how the handle works as a lever, as do the bristles of the brush. The levers allow painters to apply paint evenly and smoothly.

Machine Math

Machines and their parts offer many opportunities for impromptu mini-math lessons. Count the number of nails or screws in a pile. Combine two piles of nuts or washers and find the total. Count the dials or knobs. As the digital numbers on the microwave tick down, count backwards with children: 10-9-8-7-6-5-4-3-2-1. When the buzzer rings, shout "Blast-off!" together.

Eclipse

"Mama, where does the sun go
When I am in my bed?"
"To the other side of the Earth,"
My Mama said.

"What happens to the moon
When I go out to play?"
"It mostly wanders in the nighttime,
It doesn't like the day."

"Will they ever crash together?
I mean, do they ever meet?"
"Yes, they do," answered Mama,
"But they don't crash, they greet."

"Greet?" I asked. "Yes," she said.
"They greet in an eclipse."
"That's very hard to say," I thought,
"With only these two lips.

Wouldn't it be better,
If everyone would say,
The sun and moon got tangled up
When they came out to play?"

Cut along dashed line and glue to a brown paper lunch bag.

Reproducible

Daytime and Nighttime Activities

You will need:

> Old magazines
>
> Scissors
>
> Photocopies of photos of family members (optional)

Cut pictures from old magazines of activities that are done during the day and those done at night. Use copies of family photographs too, if you have them. Put all the pictures in one pile. Have children sort the daytime activities from those done at night.

Trace the Walking Shadow

You will need:

> White, red, and blue sidewalk chalk
>
> Chair or other large object

Early in the day, place a chair or other large object outside where the sun will shine on it for several hours. Have children trace the shadow of the object with white chalk. Wait about two hours and let children trace the shadow again with blue chalk. Have them be careful not to smudge the first drawing. Repeat the procedure with the red chalk about two hours later.

Talk about what happened to the object's shadow.

> Did the object move?
>
> How did the shadow move if the object did not move?
>
> What does the sun have to do with shadows?
>
> Where do shadows go when it is dark?

Fun Ideas to Share with Children

On the outside of this bag you will find the poem *Eclipse*. Read the poem aloud with children.

As a special treat, let children stay up past their usual bedtime. Spend time together watching the moon and stars.

Make Sun, Moon, and Star Patterns

You will need:

> Yellow construction paper
>
> Scissors

Cut large crescent moons, stars, and sun shapes from yellow construction paper. Make at least 10 of each, exactly the same. Use the shapes to make repetitive patterns:

> *moon, moon, sun, moon, moon, sun . . .*
>
> *sun, star, moon, sun, star, moon . . .*

Have children continue the pattern by correctly placing additional sun, moon, and star shapes in order. Make two, three, or four pattern sequences depending upon children's ability. Let children make their own patterns with the sun, moon, and star shapes.

Sun, Moon, and Stars Art

Let children use the sun, moon, and star shapes from the last activity and glue them to a sheet of black paper to make a nighttime collage. Add a small dab of glue to each star and sprinkle glitter over it. When glue is dry, shake the excess glitter back into the container.

Shadow Dance

You will need:

    White bed sheet
    Thumbtacks
    Radio, or tape or CD player
    Lamp

Hang a white sheet across a doorway using thumbtacks. Have children turn on a light in the room behind the sheet. Turn off all lights in the other rooms. Play a tape or CD, or turn the radio to a music station and encourage children to shadow dance behind the sheet with the light at their backs. You can be the audience or take your turn shadow dancing.

Shadow Play

Give children flashlights and darken the room. Have them shine the flashlights on a variety of objects and notice how the objects block the light and create shadows. Have them move the flashlight so its shines from different directions on the same object. What happens to the object's shadow?

Talk about how the sun is like a flashlight. When objects block the sunlight, they create shadows. What happens when the sun shines from a different angle?

Sun Puzzle

You will need:

    Large sheet of paper
    Crayons or markers
    Glue or glue stick
    Lightweight cardboard
    Scissors
    Resealable sandwich bag

Let children draw and color a large sun on a large sheet of paper. Glue the sun to lightweight cardboard. Cut the sun picture into as many puzzle pieces as children can manage to assemble successfully. Remember, if the sun picture is entirely yellow, it will be more difficult to put the puzzle pieces together. Store the puzzle pieces in a resealable sandwich bag so children can make the puzzle again and again.

What Rhymes with *Moon*?

Sun, *moon*, and *star* are good words for children to use for poems because they each have many words that rhyme. Help children think of words that rhyme with *moon*, then with *sun* and *star*. Encourage children to use two-syllable words, like *baboon*, *racoon*, and *guitar*.

Make up short poems using the words *moon*, *sun*, or *star*, and words that rhyme. Examples:

    I heard the moon sing a happy tune.

    I'd travel to a star, but it's much too far.

    We played in the sun and had lots of fun.

Wish Upon a Star

"Star light, star bright, first star I see tonight. I wish I may, I wish I might, have the wish I wish tonight." Ask children what they would wish for if they could have only one wish. Let them write or dictate a story about a child who wishes upon a star, and tell what happens. Does the wish come true? Was it a good wish?

Read the story of Pinocchio to the children. What does Pinocchio's father wish for? What does Pinocchio wish for? Do they get their wishes?

Make Moon Rocks

You will need:

> 8-ounce paper cups
> Vermiculite
> Water
> Plaster of Paris
> Paint stir stick
> Large bucket
> Heavy-duty plastic knives and spoons

Mix one part plaster of Paris, one part water, and one and a half parts vermiculite in a large bucket. Stir well with a paint stick. Pour mixture into paper cups. Set aside and allow to dry. (It will take about five days.)

Let children remove the hardened mixture from the cups and carve their own "moon rocks" using heavy-duty plastic knives and spoons.

Explore the Moon

Drape large sheets, blankets, and/or tablecloths over boxes, chairs, or stools of different heights. Leave room between items for children to crawl through. Tell children to pretend they are on the moon where everyone lives underground. Let them explore the moon by crawling under the "surface."

What If?

Ask children, "What if you could visit the moon, the sun, or another star?" Have them draw pictures showing what they think such a trip would be like.

Faces

What's on a face?
What shows there?
Two ears that hear
Overlooked by hair.

Two eyes with lashes
That see and blink.
Above? Furry eyebrows
To wiggle, I think.

There's only one nose
Pushed outward to smell.
It also makes sneezes,
Which it does very well.

Two lips and a mouth
That nibbles around.
Lips up say, "Smile!"
And down, say "Frown."

There are two cheeks
At both ends of a grin.
And then the face stops
At a point called the chin.

Some faces are round,
While others are square.
Most faces express
What our feelings put there.

Cut along dashed line and glue to a brown paper lunch bag.

Reproducible

Fun Ideas to Share with Children

Clown Faces

You will need:

Different kinds and colors of old makeup (Or purchase clown makeup at a costume rental store.)

Ask children to draw pictures of clown faces they would like to wear. Place children in front of a mirror so they can watch while you apply makeup. Try to make the faces as close as possible to the pictures drawn.

When you finish, let children compare their made-up faces to the ones they drew. How are they alike? How are they different? Talk about how it feels to wear makeup. Let children act out how the clowns they drew would act as a real clowns.

Take photos of the children wearing their clown faces to keep in your photo album.

Match Facial Expressions

Make a facial expression that expresses an emotion. Ask children to make the same expression. Use a range of emotions, like anger, sadness, happiness, fear, excitement, and surprise. As children match your facial expressions have them identify the emotion you are expressing.

On the outside of this bag you will find the poem *Faces*. Read the poem aloud with children.

Remind children that faces come in many colors, sizes, and shapes. Some faces have freckles and some are hairy. Some are smooth and some are wrinkly. Each face is unique.

Silhouettes

You will need:

Masking tape
Bright lamp
Scissors
Resealable sandwich bag
3 large sheets of white paper

Turn a lamp so the light is directed at a blank wall. Place children in front of the light. Attach white paper to the wall with masking tape to capture the shadow on the wall. Trace around the shadow and cut out three copies. Write the date on the back of one and keep it for later years in a photo album.

Use one for a puzzle by gluing it to lightweight cardboard and cutting it into simple puzzle pieces. Let children use the third silhouette as a guide to assemble the puzzle. Children will enjoy making their very own face puzzle over and over again. Store the pieces in a resealable sandwich bag.

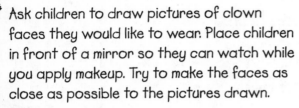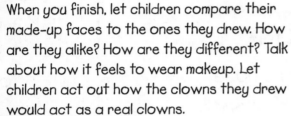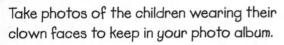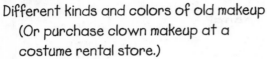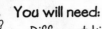

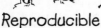

Paper-Plate Faces

You will need:
    Construction paper
    Short lengths of yarn
    Scissors
    Glue or glue stick
    Paper plate

Cut geometric shapes from construction paper (circles, crescents, triangles, ovals, squares, rectangles, semi-circles). Cut different lengths of yarn.

Let children arrange the geometric shapes and yarn on a paper plate to make faces. When items are arranged the way they want, let children glue them in place. Encourage creativity. The faces do not need to look like real people.

Facial Expressions on a Mirror

You will need:
    Washable markers
    Large mirror
    Window cleaner
    Paper towels

Let children experiment making different facial expressions in front of a large mirror. Let them draw on the mirror using washable markers, copying their facial expression in the mirror. Encourage children to draw expressions that reflect different emotions. As children draw, talk about what they see in the mirror and how a person would feel who has that expression. The drawings are easily cleaned off with window cleaner and paper towels.

Self-Portraits

You will need:
    Crayons
    Paper
    Pencil or pen

Let children draw pictures of themselves. As they draw, ask children to talk about their self-portraits. Write down thoughts and comments they make while doing the self-portraits. Save the self-portraits and what you wrote to share with children when they get older.

Feelings and Faces

Let children demonstrate different feelings, like surprise, joy, pride, delight, anger, fear, fright, happiness, and sadness. Talk about how faces look when people show different feelings.

Choose a song familiar to you and the children, like "Twinkle, Twinkle, Little Star." Sing along with the children using first a sad voice, then a happy voice. Sing fearfully, then angrily. Finally, sing in a scared voice. Encourage children to sing with you using the same expressions. Laugh a lot while you enjoy this unusual sing-along.

Match Feelings to Incidents

You will need:
    Old magazines
    Scissors
    Paper
    Crayons or markers

Cut pictures from magazines of people showing emotions, like a surprised child, a happy grandparent, or a scared teenager. Ask children to draw an incident or scene that would be appropriate for one of the expressions shown. For example, the photo of a happy grandparent might go with a scene showing a newborn baby.

Beanbag Toss

You will need:
    Large cardboard box
    Markers
    Beanbags
    Scissors or a sharp knife

Make beanbags by partially filling an old sock with dried beans and tying it securely. Cut off excess material.

Draw a large simple face on one side of the box. Cut out large holes for the eyes, nose, and mouth. Have children stand several feet away and throw beanbags at the holes in the face.

You can write a number between one and four near each hole in the box if you want to keep score, or simply add one point each time a beanbag goes through a hole.

Paper-Plate Face Masks

You will need:
    Paper plate
    Crayons or markers
    Scissors
    Hole punch
    String
    Glue or glue stick
    Yarn, ribbon, cotton balls, and paper scraps for
        decorations

Cut holes in paper plates for childrens' eyes and mouths. Let children decorate the back of the plate with crayons or markers. They can glue on yarn, ribbon, cotton balls, and paper scraps for hair and ears. Wind strips of construction paper tightly around a pencil to make curls.

Punch a small hole on both sides of each mask. Tie a 10" (25-cm) piece of string to each hole. Use the string to tie each mask in place.

© Fearon Teacher Aids FE211003

Wiggly, Fuzzy Caterpillar

A wiggly, fuzzy caterpillar
Crawled up upon my shoe,
And shouted to me clearly,
"I don't believe it's true!"

Then the wiggly, fuzzy caterpillar
Crawled up my blue-jean pants.
In a very puzzled tone he asked,
"Does it happen to the ants?"

"What did you say?" I asked him.
He pursed his lips and cried,
"Not too long from now, you know,
I'll be butterflied!"

Cut along dashed line and glue to a brown paper lunch bag.

33

Fun Ideas to Share with Children

Butterfly Dance

Spend time with children observing butterflies as they float, swoop, and flitter from flower to flower. Let children dance to music using colored scarves as butterfly wings as they imitate the motions of butterflies. Music from "The Nutcracker Suite" is great butterfly dancing music. If you don't have that music, you may be able to borrow a tape or CD from your local library.

Butterfly or Caterpillar Sculpture

You will need:

    2 cups sand
    1 cup cornstarch
    1 cup water
    Food coloring (optional)

Mix ingredients and stir well. Add a few drops of food coloring. Have an adult cook the mixture over medium heat until it thickens. Allow it to cool. At first it will be very pliable, but it will start to harden after two or three hours.

While it is pliable, children can mold the sand-clay into the form of a caterpillar or butterfly sculpture.

Symmetry

As children look at pictures of butterflies, point out how the pattern on both wings is the same. This is called *symmetry*. Help children look for other items with symmetry. A face has symmetry. Our bodies have symmetry.

On the outside of this bag you will find the poem *Wiggly, Fuzzy Caterpillar*. Read the poem aloud with children.

Explain to children that a cocoon and a chrysalis are very similar, but not the same. A cocoon is spun by a moth caterpillar and a chrysalis is spun by a butterfly caterpillar. The process of changing from a caterpillar to a butterfly or moth is called *metamorphosis*.

From a Chrysalis Comes a Butterfly

It's difficult to find a cocoon or chrysalis, but if you and the children search carefully among flowers and plants outside, you may be lucky enough to spot one. If you do, isolate it, and watch the butterfly or moth develop and emerge from its cocoon.

Check your local library for children's reference books with illustrations of the process. Study the pictures with the children. Have children make drawings of a butterfly or moth developing in, and emerging from, a cocoon or chrysalis.

The Life Cycle of a Butterfly

After learning about the life cycle of a butterfly, children can dramatize the process. First, they can roll up in a ball to represent the egg. Then they can crawl around like a caterpillar. Next they can become a chrysalis and stay very still. Finally, they can pretend to fly like a butterfly.

Butterfly Puzzle

You will need:

    White construction paper
    Crayons or markers
    Scissors
    Resealable sandwich bag

Cut large butterfly shapes from white construction paper. Have children decorate the butterflies with crayons or markers. Cut the shape into as many puzzle pieces as children can manage. Help children make the butterfly puzzle. Store the pieces in a resealable sandwich bag for use again another time.

If I Were a Caterpillar

Ask children to imagine they are talking caterpillars. What would they say? Have them tell you what it's like to be a caterpillar. Ask them how they feel about spinning a chrysalis. How do they feel about turning into a butterfly? Have children tell a story about an adventure they might have if they were a caterpillar.

Eyedropper Art on Napkins

You will need:

    Large dinner-size paper napkins, solid color if possible
    Eyedroppers
    Food coloring
    Water
    Small jars or plastic buckets (Baby food jars or yogurt containers work well.)

Cover the work area with newspaper. Fill the containers about half full of water and add a few drops of food coloring. Use several different colors or mix two colors to make new ones.

Let children fill the eyedroppers with colored water, then release the drops on the folded napkins. When the water dries, children can unfold the napkins to find a colorful surprise.

Note: Food coloring can be difficult to remove from clothing and other surfaces. Be sure children wear old "paint clothes" and work areas are covered whenever food coloring is used in an activity.

3-D Butterflies

You will need:

> Empty toilet-paper tube
> Construction paper or scraps of wallpaper
> Pipe cleaner
> Scissors
> Tape
> Crayons or markers
> Yarn or string

Cut construction paper or wallpaper to fit around the cardboard tube. Let children cover the tube with paper and tape it in place. This will be the butterfly's body.

Cut two butterfly wing shapes from construction paper or wallpaper. Let children decorate the wings with crayons or markers. Attach the wings to the body with tape.

Punch two small holes in one end of the tube with sharp-pointed scissors. Push one end of a pipe cleaner into one hole and back out through the second hole. Twist the pipe cleaner together at the base so it doesn't slip out. Pull the ends of the pipe cleaner apart. Let children bend the ends of the pipe cleaners to form the butterfly's antennae. Hold in place with tape, if needed.

Insert string or yarn through the tube and tie the ends together to make a hanger for your butterfly.

A Caterpillar Riddle

Ask children this riddle: *What kind of insect holds up a building?*

> Answer: *A cater-pillar!*

Have children make up their own caterpillar and butterfly riddles and see if you can answer them.

The Very Hungry Caterpillar

Check out the book *The Very Hungry Caterpillar* by Eric Carle from the library. It is a delightful story of a caterpillar eating lots and lots of leaves every day before changing into a butterfly. Read the book out loud with children. While you are at the library, look for nonfiction books about butterflies and moths.

Egg-Carton Caterpillar

You will need:

> Egg carton
> Tape or glue
> Markers
> String
> Bead or button
> 2 pipe cleaners
> Scissors
> Hole punch
> Markers

Cut the bottom of an egg carton in half the long way so you have two six-cup sections. Punch one hole in one end of each six-cup section. Let children fasten the two sections together and turn them upside down to make one long caterpillar.

At the "head" of the caterpillar, punch two holes in the egg cup. Have children insert a pipe cleaner into one hole and back out the other to make the caterpillar's antennae.

Children can add facial details to the caterpillar and decorate its body with markers.

To make a pull-toy caterpillar, punch a hole in the head section about halfway down. Put a long piece of string through the hole and tie a knot so the string doesn't slip out. Tie a bead or button to the other end of the string. Children can pull their caterpillars around by the string.

Globe

A map of the world,
Laid out flat
Would not be a globe,
As a matter of fact.

But it could be, though,
If rolled in a ball.
Then it would be a globe
With no corners at all.

Covered with land, and
Rivers, and trees,
And mountains, and oceans
Whipped by a breeze.

In some places it's rainy,
And in others it's dry.
It's hard to imagine,
But you can, if you try.

You can see shapes,
And colors and lines.
Can you name places
Your fingers can find?

Cut along dashed line and glue to a brown paper lunch bag.

37

Reproducible

Paint a Globe Made from Newspaper

You will need:

- Wallpaper paste
- Large pan or bowl
- Newspaper
- Round balloon
- Washable paint
- Paintbrush

Tear several sheets of newspaper into strips two to three inches (5 cm to 7.5 cm) wide. Blow up a round balloon. Mix wallpaper paste in a large pan or bowl.

Let children place the newspaper strips in the paste. Cover the balloon with newspaper strips one at a time, winding the strips around and around to cover the entire balloon. Let dry overnight.

Repeat the process the next day until the balloon is covered with many layers of newspaper. When the balloon is thoroughly dry, insert a pin into it through the newspaper. The air will escape, leaving a large ball children can paint to resemble a globe.

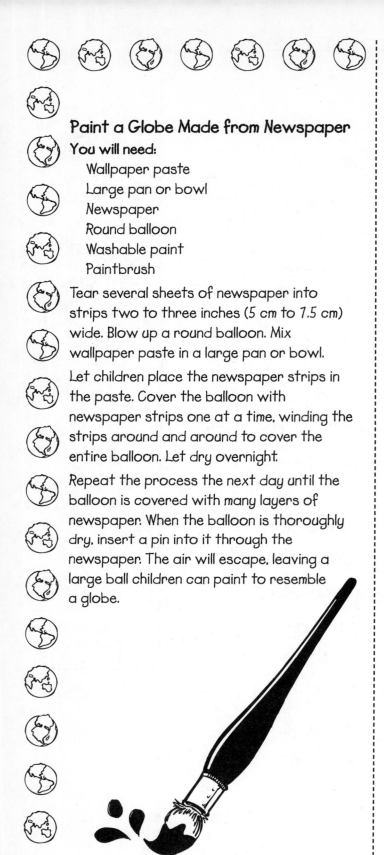

Fun Ideas to Share with Children

On the outside of this bag you will find the poem *Globe*. Read the poem aloud with children.

If you don't have a globe of the earth, use a spinning top to help children understand how the earth spins on its axis. The spinning of the earth is called *rotation*.

Compare a World Map and a Globe

Show children a flat map of the world and a globe. Talk about how the flat map and the globe are the same and how they are different. Help children find continents and oceans on the map, then locate them on the globe.

Discover the Key

You will need:

- Atlas (book of maps)
- Globe
- City, state, or local maps

Help children become familiar with the types of information found on maps. Some maps show where minerals are found; where certain foods are grown; or where famous sites, mountains, deserts, forests, and oceans are located. Share maps with children. Search together to find items shown on the map key. A map key shows symbols for items found on the map. Point out a symbol on the map key, like the one that represents *mountains*. Then find that symbol on the map.

Pillowcase Globe

You will need:

Large ball (like a beach ball or basketball)
Old pillowcase
Markers
Twist tie or string
Crayons, markers, or paints and paintbrush

Have children make their own globes of the world, by stuffing a large ball into an old pillowcase. Use a twist tie or string to close the pillowcase. Decorate the pillowcase with markers, paints, or crayons to look like a globe.

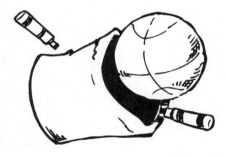

Globe (Circle) Books

You will need:

Cardboard
Paper
Stapler

Cut two large circles from lightweight cardboard. You can trace around a dinner plate to make the circle. Cut several sheets of paper in circles using the cardboard as a pattern. Staple the paper between the cardboard covers to make a book. Have children write a story telling about the globe they made with newspapers and a balloon or with a pillowcase and a ball. Children often use invented spelling at this age. It is more important for them to know they are successful writers than it is for them to spell words correctly at this point.

It's a Small World

You will need:

Words to the song "It's a Small World" (The library should be able to help you find this.)

Teach children the song and sing it together. Talk about what the writer of the song was saying about the world. Is it really small? Is it really large? In what ways is the world large? What makes it seem small?

Follow Map Trails

You will need:

City or neighborhood map
Variety of maps showing walking or driving routes to local sites like a zoo, botanical gardens, parks, and wilderness areas
Clear adhesive paper
Washable marker

Have the maps laminated or cover them with clear adhesive paper. Let children follow the paths with a washable marker. Wipe off and reuse as often as you like.

Make several photocopies of a map of your city or neighborhood. (You can often find one in the telephone book.) Help children locate the place on the map where they live and the route to places they visit frequently, like school, shopping malls, the post office, doctor or dentist's offices, and homes of friends and relatives.

Glue

I was busy gluing

Some paper to a stick.

I squeezed the tube too hard.

The glue came out too quick.

It poured right down my fingers.

It dripped upon the table.

I used my shirt to wipe it—

As much as I was able.

My shirt stuck to the paper

And the paper stuck to me.

I stuck to the table.

There we were, all three,

Captured by a gooey mess,

By sticky stuff that's strong,

Rightly stuck together,

Even when it's wrong!

Cut along dashed line and glue to a brown paper lunch bag.

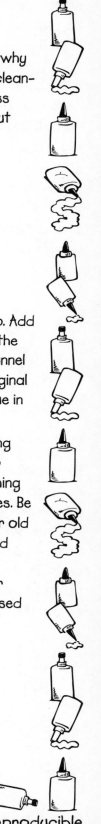

Egg-White Glue

Let children experiment using egg white as glue. Apply it with a cotton swab or artist's paintbrush. It is very sticky. Add food coloring for more fun!

Glue Sun Catchers

You will need:

- Clear plastic lids
- Colored glue (from "Colored Glue" activity)
- String or yarn
- Hole punch

Recycle clear plastic tops from yogurt cups and coffee cans by letting children draw on them with colored glue. It takes a day or two for the glue to dry thoroughly. When it is dry, peel off the colored design, punch a hole in the lid, and hang it in the window for a sun catcher.

Rubbings with Glue

You will need:

- Colored glue (from "Colored Glue" activity)
- Construction paper or lightweight cardboard
- Crayon with wrapper removed

Have children draw a picture or design on construction paper or lightweight cardboard with colored glue. Let glue dry completely. Have children lay white paper over the glue picture and rub over it with the side of a crayon. Examine the crayon drawing and compare it to the original picture drawn with glue.

Fun Ideas to Share with Children

On the outside of this bag you will find the poem *Glue*. Read the poem aloud with children.

Glue is sticky and messy. Maybe that's why kids love it. Buy only washable glue, so clean-up is quick and easy. Glue sticks are less messy and easier for children to use, but won't work for all activities.

Colored Glue

You will need:

- 4-ounce bottle of white glue
- Food coloring
- Craft stick
- Funnel
- Large paper cup

Empty white glue into a large paper cup. Add about 20 drops of food coloring. Stir the mixture well with a craft stick. Use a funnel to pour the contents back into the original glue bottle. Make several bottles of glue in different colors.

Note: Food coloring can be difficult to remove from clothing and other surfaces. Be sure children wear old "paint clothes" and work areas are covered whenever food coloring is used in an activity.

Removable Pictures

You will need:

- Sticky notes (or a stick of removable glue and 2" x 2" [5 cm x 5 cm] paper squares)
- Crayons and markers
- Blunt scissors
- Posterboard

Ask children to draw several pictures of activities or events on separate sticky notes or paper squares. The pictures can show actions that go together or objects used or found together (like several types of flowers, gardening tools, fish, farm animals, and so on).

If the pictures are drawn on paper, have children cut them out with a blunt scissors. Apply the removable glue to the back of the paper. Applying the glue makes the paper work like sticky notes, making the paper sticky, but movable. Have children arrange and rearrange the pictures on posterboard to show events in different sequences, stories, or scenes.

Glue and Shake

You will need:

- White glue or colored glue (from "Colored Glue" activity)
- Construction paper or lightweight cardboard
- Box lid larger than the paper
- Empty cheese shaker box or other shaker that can be filled
- Sawdust, confetti, sand, glitter, cornmeal, uncooked rice, bird seed, grit, or Epsom salts

Fill a shaker with one of the materials listed above. Have children place a sheet of construction paper or lightweight cardboard in the box lid and draw on it with glue. Before the glue dries, have children shake one of the materials listed onto their pictures. When glue dries, shake excess material off in the box top. The material stuck to the glue will remain.

Silly Dough

You will need:

- 1 tablespoon liquid starch
- 2 tablespoons glue
- Empty plastic container
- Resealable sandwich bag

Mix liquid starch and glue in a small plastic container. Stir and knead mixture until the starch is absorbed and it is smooth—the more mixing the better. Wipe off the excess starch. If mixture is stringy, place it in a resealable sandwich bag overnight and try again the next day. If it is not mixing well, add a bit more starch. Place mixture in a resealable sandwich bag overnight. The next day you can use your Silly Dough for bouncy, gooey fun.

Glue Dough

You will need:

- 3/4 cup flour
- 1/4 cup glue
- 1/4 cup thick shampoo
- Washable paints
- Paintbrushes

Mix ingredients and knead well. If mixture is too sticky, add a little more flour. Children can roll out the Glue Dough to make pancake shapes, model with it, or roll it into "snakes."

Help children roll the Glue Dough flat and press a hand firmly into it to make a permanent handprint model. Make a small hole at the top of the handprint with a toothpick and thread ribbon through the hole. Tie a bow in the ribbon for a hanger. After models dry, children can paint them with washable paints.

Glue Molds

This recipe makes a liquid that pours easily into different shape molds and has a marble look when dry.

- 2 teaspoons glue
- 1/2 cup water
- Plaster of Paris
- 1/4 cup washable paint
- Molds (*see below)

Mix glue and water. Stir in plaster of Paris to make a creamy mixture. Cover the top of the mixture with 1/4 cup of paint. Stir the paint into the mixture so it streaks, giving it a marble effect. Pour into a mold and allow to dry.

*Children can pour the mixture into candy molds, small plastic containers, milk cartons, or paper cups. Several shapes can be glued together to make a construction design. Try a variety of molds.

3-D Glue Sculpture

You will need:

- 1/2 cup liquid starch
- 2 cups rock salt
- 1/2 cup glue
- Food coloring (optional)
- Lightweight cardboard
- Cotton swabs

Combine ingredients to make a gooey mixture. Pile it on a sheet of lightweight cardboard with a cotton swab to make three-dimensional free-form designs. Let designs dry.

Lemonade

The sourest pucker I ever made

Was when my mother made lemonade.

I grabbed a lemon from next to the sink.

I took a bite. My last, I think.

I couldn't breathe for a minute or two.

My poor eyes watered.
My tongue turned blue.

My two cheeks quivered and
sucked in tight.

I couldn't unstick them, try as I might.

Mother noticed very quickly

That my face looked very sickly.

She gave me water with sugar in it.

I drank it down in less than a minute.

If you're smart you'll follow this advice:

Mix your lemons with sugar, water, and ice.

From now on I'll take Mom's first-aid.

And only drink unpuckered lemonade!

Cut along dashed line and glue to a brown paper lunch bag.

Experiment with Taste

Try the following taste experiment using the scientific method.

1. **State a question:** Does the taste of one food affect the taste of another?

2. **Predict the results:** Ask children to predict what will happen.

3. **Do the experiment:** Try tasting foods in different order to see if the taste of one food affects the taste of another.

   For example: Have children eat a small piece of lemon, then a small piece of chocolate. Does the chocolate taste as sweet as usual?

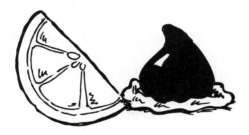

4. **Determine the results:** Have children tell what they learned from the experiment.

Let children make up other science questions and taste experiments to answer the questions, like trying two foods at once or tasting food when they have a cold.

Fun Ideas to Share with Children

On the outside of this bag you will find the poem *Lemonade*. Read the poem aloud with children.

Ask children to pretend they have just eaten a very sour slice of lemon. Ask them to show you their best puckers.

Unpuckered Lemonade

Children can make "unpuckered" lemonade with this recipe.

You will need:

    12-ounce plastic glass
    1/4 lemon
    Sugar cube or teaspoon of sugar
    Ice
    Water

Squeeze the juice from a quartered lemon into the glass. Add sugar, water, and ice. Stir and enjoy.

While children enjoy drinking their lemonade, review the steps they took to make it. Later, ask them to draw pictures showing each step, in the order they followed to make lemonade.

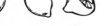

Three Taste Treats: Salty, Sour, and Sweet
You will need:

Foods from the three taste groups: salty, sour, and sweet

Sweet: jelly beans, gum, chocolate, sugar cube

Sour: dill pickles, candy sour-balls, lemon or lime slices

Salty: crackers, pretzels, popcorn

Let children taste foods from the three major groups, one at a time. Discuss which foods they like and which ones they don't like.

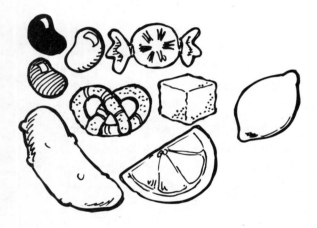

Lemon-Juice Freeze
You will need:

Lemon or orange-juice squeezer

Empty ice-cube tray

Lemon halves

Sugar (or sweetener)

Have children squeeze the lemon halves over the ice-cube tray until the juice is squeezed out. Use enough lemons to fill the ice tray about 3/4 full. Put the ice-cube tray in the freezer overnight. Place one lemon cube in a glass. Add a teaspoon of sugar (or sweetener) and water. Stir and drink.

If children have any cuts on their hands, they should not squeeze lemons. The juice will sting.

Lemon Notes
You will need:

Lightweight cardboard

Yellow paper

Blunt scissors

Stapler

Cut a lemon shape from lightweight cardboard for a pattern. Have children trace around the pattern on yellow paper and cut the shapes with blunt scissors. Staple several lemon-shaped sheets together to make a lemon notepad. Encourage children to write notes to you and other family members. Children at this age often use invented spelling. It is more important for them to know they are successful writers than it is for them to spell words correctly at this point.

If You Were a Lemon
Ask children to imagine what it would be like to be a talking lemon. Ask them to give reasons why people should buy them. Remember, most people think lemons are sour, so children will need to be convincing.

Lemon Squares

Cooking is fun for young children. Let them help you make lemon squares for desert or an after-school snack.

You will need:

Crust

3/4 cup cold butter

1/3 cup powdered sugar

1 1/2 cups flour

Mix ingredients together. They will form a crumbly pastry. Line a 9" x 13" (22.5 cm x 32.5 cm) baking pan with the crumbly pastry mix. Bake at 350 degrees for 20 minutes.

You will need:

Filling

6 slightly beaten eggs

3 cups sugar

6 tablespoons flour

8 tablespoons lemon juice

Mix ingredients thoroughly with a spoon. Pour the filling over the crust. Bake for 20 minutes at 350 degrees. Sprinkle powdered sugar on top. Cut into squares when cool.

Put Lemons in Order by Size

You will need:

5 lemons of different sizes

Have children put the lemons in order by size, from largest to smallest. Talk about how items that are the same, like lemons, apples, pumpkins, and people come in different sizes. Ask children to name other things that are the same but come in different sizes.

Yellow Collage

You will need:

Many small yellow items (like paper, cloth, yarn, ribbons, bows, stickers, buttons, and pictures of yellow objects)

Glue or glue stick

Yellow paper plate (If you only have white, use yellow markers, crayons, or paint to color it yellow.)

Have children arrange the yellow objects and pictures on a yellow paper plate and glue them in place. Hang collages in a prominent place for all to enjoy.

A Lemon Riddle

Ask children this riddle: *What would you get if your cat ate a lemon?*

Answer: *A sour puss!*

Encourage children to make up their own lemon riddles.

Use Your Senses to Learn About Lemons

Write the words *look, feel, taste, smell,* and *hear* inside five large circles. Have children use their senses to learn about lemons. Write the descriptive words they use inside the appropriate circles.

Show children a lemon. Let them examine it closely. Cut it in half for further observation. Are there any seeds? Does the inside of a lemon look more like an orange or an apple? Ask children to describe what they see.

Have children smell the lemon. What words can they use to describe how the lemon smells?

Have children taste the lemon and describe how it tastes.

How does the lemon feel? Does the outside feel the same as the inside? How do the seeds feel?

Listen to the lemon. Does it make any sounds? What sounds do they hear when you squeeze the lemon?

Talk about how we learn about the world around us by using our eyes, hands, mouth, nose, and ears. Explore other objects in the same manner.

Lemon Storybooks

You will need:
Yellow construction paper
Writing paper
Scissors
Stapler

Make covers for a "Lemon Book" by cutting two lemon shapes from yellow construction paper. Cut several sheets of writing paper by using one of the covers as a pattern. Staple pages together between covers.

Have children write and illustrate a story about what it would be like to be a lemon in their "Lemon Books." After children finish the books, help them read their stories several times.

Lemon Fractions

Start with a whole lemon. Cut it in half. Explain to children that halves are two equal parts. Let children put the two halves back together so they can see that there is still the same amount of lemon as before.

Cut the lemon halves again. Explain to children that when something is cut into four equal parts, the parts are called *fourths*. Ask children to give you 1/4 of the lemon, then 3/4 of the lemon.

Have children put two of the quarters together. Ask them how much of a lemon they have. Explain that two quarters equals one-half.

Have them put the four quarters back together so they can see that four quarters equals one whole.

My Little Brother

I have a little brother
Who says he wants to learn
How to be grown-up like me
And how to take his turn.

I shared my brand-new telescope.
He dropped it in the grass.
He looked into it backwards,
Then he fogged up all the glass.

I helped him do construction
With some blocks we had around.
He stacked them up so tumbly,
That they knocked my building down.

When we play hide and seek
And it's his turn to find,
He forgets to look for me,
But I do not really mind.

'Cause when Mama says, "It's bedtime!"
After being bathed and fed,
It's not so dark and scary
Since we share a nice big bed.

Cut along dashed line and glue to a brown paper lunch bag.

Fun Ideas to Share with Children

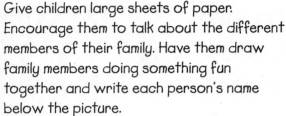

Family Portraits

Give children large sheets of paper. Encourage them to talk about the different members of their family. Have them draw family members doing something fun together and write each person's name below the picture.

My, How You've Changed!

Gather several photos of the children at different ages, going back to when they were babies. Show them the photos and talk about what they were like at each age. Tell them about funny things they did when they were smaller, or about the first time they took a step alone. Children enjoy hearing stories about themselves "when they were little."

Have children compare how they look now to how they looked in earlier photos. Ask them to point out ways they are the same and ways they have changed.

Children often have difficulty understanding that their parents were once children who had parents of their own. If you have pictures of yourself as a child, share them with the children. Look for ways your children resemble you when you were a child.

A Family Record of Height

Use a roll of adding-machine paper (or several sheets of paper taped together) cut to the height of each family member. Attach the paper to the wall with masking tape. Write each person's height and name on the appropriate strip. Ask children to compare the heights. Who is tallest? shortest? Who is in the middle?

On the outside of this bag you will find the poem *My Little Brother.* Read the poem aloud with children.

Children usually have mixed feelings about their brothers and sisters. Sometimes they get along great, and other times they seem to disagree on everything.

Your Family in Photographs

Gather old family photographs (going back in time as far as possible).

Show children the photographs and help them identify the family members in the pictures. Talk about the relationships between members. Share what you remember about them and activities you did together. Let children help organize your photo albums.

Family Picnic

Allow children to plan a family picnic (at a park or in the backyard). Children can help prepare and pack food for the picnic. Let them plan several activities your family can do together. In winter, or if the weather is bad, have your family picnic on a blanket on the living-room floor.

Ask each family member to take turns completing this sentence:

Our family is special because . . .

Your Family Tree

Make a family tree with copies of photographs. Draw a large tree. Place the pictures in the branches. Talk about how the people are related to each other and to the children. Explain words like *aunt*, *uncle*, and *cousin*.

Use Graphs to Compare

Help children graph the number of family members in your household, your neighbor's household, and a friend's. Talk about the differences in the numbers of family members.

My Family	☺	‖‖‖	3
Sam's Family	☺	‖‖‖‖‖	5
Aunt Sara's Family	☺	‖‖	2

Family Clothing Sort

When doing the laundry, have children help sort clothes by size for members of the family. Use one laundry basket for each family member and let children put the clothing in the appropriate basket.

Compare articles of clothing. Whose shirt is the largest? Whose socks are the smallest? Which two people have clothing that is almost alike?

When the laundry is finished, let children help sort socks by looking for matching pairs. Roll the pairs into balls and let children have a sock toss. They can toss the pairs into a laundry basket. Even if they miss, praise them for their efforts: "That was a good throw," or "Pretty close. Try again."

Family Voices

Find photographs of each member of your family. If possible, include relatives who do not live in your home. Have each family member speak into a tape recorder, describing activities they like to do. Have children match the voices to the photographs.

Family Puzzle

Use a copy of a family photograph to make a puzzle. Glue the photo to lightweight cardboard. Cut the photograph into as many pieces as you think children can assemble successfully. Let them make the puzzle as often as they like. Save the pieces in a resealable sandwich bag for use again later.

Family Photo Album

Staple several sheets of paper between two pieces of cardboard. Lightly write the words *Our Family* on the front cover in pencil. Let children trace the letters in crayon or marker and add other decorations to the cover.

Ask children to draw a picture of each family member on a separate page and write the person's name below the picture. Have them include family members who do not live in your household, like grandparents, aunts, uncles, and cousins. If you have extra photos, attach a picture of each person to the drawing so children will have their own family photo albums.

Play Clay Families

Let children make models of each person in the family using clay. They can form the clay to make three-dimensional figures or flatten the clay and use people-shaped cookie cutters. When they have completed their own families, they can make other family groups.

Talk about what makes a family and how families are not all the same. Families can have only a mom or a dad or include grandparents and other relatives. Some families include adopted or foster children. Some families have many children, and some have only one.

Reproducible

My Ears

My ears, my ears, my ears!

They don't know how they hear.

The sound goes in and rattles about,

But where in the world does
the sound come out?

Cut along dashed line and glue to a brown paper lunch bag.

Listen with a Stethoscope

You will need:

Stethoscope (Stethoscopes can be purchased at a medical supply house for about $5.)

Stethoscopes are great for young children to use under supervision. They will listen to everything! Have children listen to sounds from the ground (see "Sounds from the Ground" activity), but this time with a stethoscope. Ask them if the sounds are different. Do they hear more sounds than they did before? Talk about how a stethoscope makes sounds much louder.

Encourage children to listen to sounds coming from their bodies. Have them try listening to walls, floors, doors, and windows of your house. (This can be especially fun when it is windy outside).

Carrot Crunch

Whenever you and the children have carrots or other crunchy foods for a snack, encourage them to listen to the sounds made when they take a bite. What sound do they hear? What else sounds crunchy like that? What makes the crunch sound?

On the outside of this bag you will find the poem *My Ears*. Read the poem aloud with children.

Talk about how ears are important because they allow us to hear many wonderful sounds, from a whispered secret to the music of a marching band.

Music Shakers

You will need:

2 small paper plates
Stapler
6 to 12 dried beans
Markers
Ribbon

Have children decorate the back of both plates with markers. Staple halfway around the edges of the two plates with front sides together. Insert the beans and staple the remaining half closed. Add ribbon streamers to the edges. Children can use their musical shakers to shake and dance to the beat of their favorite songs.

Sounds from the Ground

On a warm, sunny day, take children outside. Have them lie down, press their ears to the ground, and listen. What do they hear? Have them describe the sounds. Ask them to tell if they think the sounds are made by people or natural events. Have them try to estimate whether the sounds are far away or close.

Talk about how sounds might travel great distances. On a clear night you may be able to hear a train many miles away. Let children listen to trees, flowers, and any other objects they are curious about.

Reproducible

My Sounds Book

You will need:

    Blank paper
    Construction paper
    Stapler
    Blunt scissors
    Old magazines and catalogs
    Glue or glue stick
    Crayons or markers

Staple several sheets of blank paper between two sheets of construction paper to make a book. Write the title *My Sounds Book* on the cover lightly in pencil. Have children trace over the letters with crayons or markers.

Have children cut out pictures of machines from old magazines and catalogs of objects that make sounds, like electrical tools, musical instruments, and appliances. Have them glue each picture to a blank page in their books.

Have children imitate the sound each object makes. Write a word or words for the sounds below the picture. Sound words do not need to be real words, they merely need to describe or imitate sounds.

Listen to Popcorn

Next time you make popcorn, encourage children to listen to the sounds of the popping corn. Talk about how the sound of the corn hitting the lid of the pot is different than the sound of the popping corn. Ask children what they think is happening inside the popper. Encourage them to act out the role of a popping kernel of corn, including the popping sounds.

House Sounds

Use a tape recorder to capture interesting sounds in your house, like the sounds of a washing machine and dryer, a ticking clock, a vacuum cleaner, a leaky faucet, a fluorescent light fixture, and other house sounds. Have children listen to the tape and try to identify the sounds. If they cannot identify a particular sound, send them on a "sound hunt" to find the source.

Talk about nighttime house sounds. How are nighttime sounds different than daytime sounds? Sit in a quiet room with children and simply listen. You may be surprised at what sounds you hear when you and the children really listen closely.

Balloon Band

You will need:

    3 balloons
    Spoonful of uncooked rice
    Spoonful of dried beans
    Spoonful of sand

Pour the uncooked rice into a balloon. Blow up the balloon and tie off the end. Do the same with the dried beans and sand. Let children shake the balloons to music. Talk about the different sounds made by the different materials in the balloons. Encourage them to think of other materials you could put in a balloon to made different sounds. Store the balloons in grocery bags in case they pop unexpectedly.

Neighborhood

"What is a neighborhood?" you ask.

Apartments, schools, parks, and paths,

Trees, birds, dogs, and cats,

Churches, friends, and welcome mats.

A place where friends meet and greet.

They park their cars along the streets.

All the streets are close to home,

The sidewalks and yards you like to roam.

"What is a neighborhood?" you say.

The places you like to go each day.

Cut along dashed line and glue to a brown paper lunch bag.

Reproducible

Neighborhood Buildings Book

Make a "Neighborhood Buildings" book by stapling several sheets of blank paper between two sheets of construction paper. Have children draw pictures of buildings in your neighborhood, one per page. On the facing page, have them write or dictate a short story about the building. The stories could be true or fiction. Read the stories back to children at bedtime.

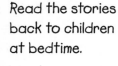
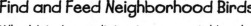

Find and Feed Neighborhood Birds

What birds are living in your neighborhood? Take a walk with children and find out. When you return, place a container of bird seed in your yard or on a windowsill. Have children observe the birds that feed in your yard. Teach children the names of the different types of birds they see. If you don't know, check your local library. You'll find many colorful books about birds.

Fun Ideas to Share with Children

On the outside of this bag you will find the poem *Neighborhood*. Read the poem aloud with children.

Take children for a walk around the neighborhood. Talk about the houses, businesses, parks, churches, open fields, empty lots, and spaces that make up a neighborhood. Ask children what part of the neighborhood they like best.

Neighborhood Map

After your walk, help children make a map of the neighborhood. Draw your street and others nearby. Mark the location of your home and other places in the neighborhood. Talk about how a map helps us find our way around. Ask children to show the way to places they visited on their walk by tracing the route on the map.

Buildings Have Texture

Have children bring several sheets of paper and a crayon without a wrapper along on a neighborhood walk. Have them place the paper on different building surfaces and use the side of the crayon to rub back and forth over the paper. The surface texture of the building will appear. Do several different textured buildings. Have children compare how the building surfaces are the same and different.

Plant a Tree

Let children plant small trees in your yard or a nearby park. Select a hearty species, native to your geographic region.

Give the tree a name and encourage children to take care of the tree as it grows. Talk about how trees provide places for birds to live, build nests, find food, and raise baby birds. Talk about how other animals and insects live in trees too.

Look at Buildings in Your Neighborhood

As you walk around your neighborhood with children, point out different features of buildings, like the kinds of doors and windows they have. Talk about the different numbers, letters, and words on buildings and what they mean. Explain how numbers and letters help people find specific buildings.

Compare buildings that are used for homes, grocery stores, apartments, banks, and restaurants. How are they the same? How are they different? What do people do in the buildings?

Build Your Neighborhood

You will need:

   A variety of empty boxes in different shapes and sizes (like the ones used to package shoes, toothpaste, soap, cereal, crackers, and other items)

Let children arrange the boxes to represent buildings in your neighborhood. Designate one box as your home and others as the homes of friends, a grocery store, pet store, library, restaurant, bank, and so on. They can take dolls, stuffed animals, and action figures for walks in the miniature neighborhood or use toy cars to take a ride.

Your Neighborhood: Then and Now

Ask a neighbor who has lived in the area for a long time to tell children how the neighborhood looked a long time ago. Encourage children to ask questions about how the neighborhood has changed, how much trees have grown, which buildings were built recently, and which old buildings were torn down. If you have a tape recorder, tape the interview to play back later. Stop! Look! Listen!

As you walk through your neighborhood with the children, encourage them to use their senses to notice things they may not have noticed before.

Look! What do they see? Have them look up, down, and around. Notice colors and shadows. Look for surfaces that are shiny or sparkling.

Listen! Have children close their eyes and listen to the sounds of your neighborhood. What do they hear? How many different sounds can they hear? Which are people sounds? Which are animal sounds? Which are machine sounds?

Smell! Have children close their eyes and concentrate on the smells of your neighborhood. What do they smell? Is someone baking cookies? Do they smell car exhaust? How many smells can they discover and identify?

Taste! What taste treats are there in your neighborhood? Is there a special restaurant or bakery where you can stop for a snack? Is one of your neighbors making his or her special recipe?

Feel! What do they feel? Let children touch various surfaces and compare their textures. Grass, glass, concrete, brick, wood, and metal are a few of the many different surfaces and textures you might find in your neighborhood.

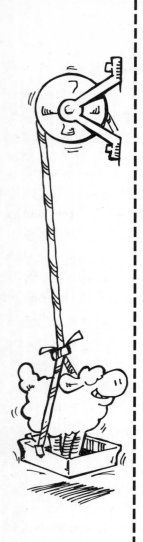

Pulley

A pulley's not woolly

Like a lamb or a sheep.

It picks things up,

And puts them down,

And stacks them in a heap.

A crane is a pulley

That arches in the air.

It picks things up here,

And puts them over there.

Cut along dashed line and glue to a brown paper lunch bag.

Many Basic Tools are Levers

A *lever* is a simple machine that allows people to lift and move objects more easily. Under supervision, let children remove a nail from a piece of wood with a claw hammer. This demonstrates how a lever works.

A shovel is another type of lever. Let children dig with a shovel to demonstrate. A wheel barrow, teeter-totter, and broom are all levers. Point out how a wheelbarrow is a lever combined with a wheel and axle.

Wheels and Axles

Turn a tricycle or bicycle upside down and show children how the wheel spins on the axle when the pedals are turned. Let children roll a wheel that is not attached to an axle. Compare the axle and wheel to the wheel alone. What is different about rolling them?

Fun Ideas to Share with Children

On the outside of this bag you will find the poem *Pulley*. Read the poem aloud with children.

Introduce children to simple machines by talking about the pulley and other simple machines, like the lever and wheel. Talk about how machines make our lives easier.

Simple machines are put together in different combinations to make complicated machines like cars, boats, trains, and airplanes. Open your car hood and show children the belt (pulley), which turns to cool your car engine and to operate other parts of the engine. The activities below will help children understand more about simple machines.

Messenger Pulley

If you are willing to make holes in the wood trim or walls of a room (like a basement or garage), you can demonstrate how a pulley works and let children have fun while learning. Purchase two 1-inch (2.5-cm) pulleys at a hardware store. (Buy the ones with the lag screws attached.) Attach one pulley to one side of the room (a corner is good) and the second pulley in the opposite corner. Run a length of nylon string from one pulley to the other and tie it off to make a pulley system.

Place a box of paper and pencils under each pulley. Encourage children to write notes and attach them to the bottom string with a clothespin. Pull or push the pulley string to move the note toward someone on the other side of the room. Read the note, write an answer, and use the pulley to send it back.

Reproducible

The Wedge as a Simple Machine

Let children examine and compare nails and wood screws. How are they alike? How are they different? Why are they different?

Screw several wood screws with large heads into a block of wood. Let children unscrew them, then screw them back in. Ask them if it would be harder or easier to push the screw in the wood with their thumbs. Under close supervision, have children try to remove a screw from a piece of wood with a claw hammer.

Point out how the shaft of the screw is tapered to enter the wood more easily when the screw is turned. The screw threads hold on to the wood as the shaft and the head are turned by the screwdriver.

Wheelbarrows as Machines

Ask children if they can spot several different simple machines that are combined to make a wheelbarrow. The wheel and axle are two simple machines that help the wheelbarrow roll.

Have children push an empty wheelbarrow. Then place an object in the wheelbarrow that normally would be too heavy for children to lift, like a 40-pound bag of potting soil. Let children push the full wheelbarrow. Point out how the handles of the wheelbarrow are like levers that allow them to lift heavy objects.

Hand Drills

Have an adult drill several holes into a block of soft pine using a hand drill and a 1/8" (3-mm) wood bit. Have children use a 1/4" (6-mm) wood bit to drill holes on top of the holes you have drilled. (Drilling over smaller holes will make drilling safer and easier for children.) Close supervision is necessary for this activity.

Ask children if they can spot several different simple machines that are combined to make a hand drill. The drill is a wheel and axle machine. The bit turns around an outside axle called a *chuck*. Your arm works as a lever by turning the drill crank. The tip of the drill bit is a wedge.

Look for Simple Machines

Look through your house, your basement, and garage with the children. How many simple machines can you and the children find? Which ones contain a combination of several simple machines? (For this purpose, ignore electrical appliances, those powered by gas, or diesel engines.)

Do you have a hand-operated can opener or eggbeater? What about a spatula or a pair of scissors? Is a stapler a machine? How about a toothbrush, comb, and hairbrush?

Hammers, shovels, rakes, hoes, screwdrivers, pliers, wrenches, hand saws, and crowbars are common tools that are simple machines. Help children learn the names of tools you have and demonstrate how to use them.

As you walk around your neighborhood, ask children to look for simple machines and machines that combine several simple machines to make more complex ones. How many can you and the children identify?

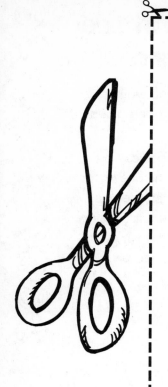

Scissors

There's scissors on the table

That I really want to use.

Finger loops are in the handle.

Which fingers? I must choose.

I open them and close them

To make the scissors go.

How do they cut the paper?

Does anybody know?

The blades do all the cutting.

That's how the work begins.

But someone needs to tell me

How to hold the paper in.

Cut along dashed line and glue to a brown paper lunch bag.

61

Reproducible

Fun Ideas to Share with Children

Cut on the Lines

Draw straight and curved lines on a large sheet of paper with a wide-point marker. Encourage children to cut along the lines.

Making the lines wide helps children be successful at cutting. This is an excellent way to improve fine motor skills and hand-eye coordination.

Things I Like

You will need:

Old magazines, catalogs, and ads
Glue or glue stick
Construction paper
Three-ring binder
Paper punched for three-ring binder

Let children cut pictures from old magazines, catalogs, and ads. They can cut out pictures of toys, babies, trees, food, games—whatever they find interesting. Let them sort the pictures into groups, like food, toys, clothing, animals, and people; or sort by color—red objects in one pile, blue ones in another, and so on.

Let children glue the pictures on paper in the three-ring binder to make a book of "Things I Like." Add more pictures or family photos whenever the opportunity arises.

On the outside of this bag you will find the poem *Scissors*. Read the poem aloud with children.

Many young children have trouble using scissors because they lack the fine motor skills needed. The more children use scissors, the better they become. Blunt scissors are recommended for young children. If your child is left-handed, be certain to provide left-handed scissors.

Snip-the-Strip Mosaic

You will need:

Paper in various colors
Blunt scissors
Small bag or container
Glue or glue stick

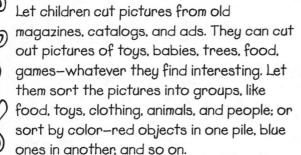

Cut 2" (5-cm) strips from scraps of colored paper or construction paper. Let children snip the strips into many small pieces. Place the cut pieces in a small bag or container. When the bag is full, let children glue the pieces to construction paper to make a mosaic design.

Pinking Shears Make Funny Edges

Let children cut with an old pair of pinking shears. They will enjoy using scissors that make "funny edges." Have them cut shapes from magazines, wallpaper, newspaper, construction paper, or scrap material.

Celebrate with a Birthday Tree

You will need:

A bare tree branch about 25" to 30" (62.5 cm to 75 cm) long, with lots of small branches extending off of it (Find one that has fallen rather than cutting one from a living tree. If it's too large, trim it with pruning shears.)

Blunt scissors

Construction paper

Empty coffee can

Small rocks

Tape

Hole punch

Thread or string

Crayons or markers

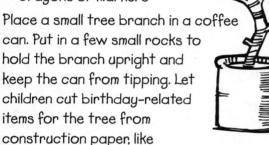

Place a small tree branch in a coffee can. Put in a few small rocks to hold the branch upright and keep the can from tipping. Let children cut birthday-related items for the tree from construction paper, like birthday candle shapes, balloon shapes, gift package shapes, a birthday cake shape, and cutout numbers to represent the person's age.

Have children decorate the shapes with crayons or markers. Use a hole punch and tie the shapes to the tree with thread, or tape them to the tree. Add a few colorful ribbons or gift-wrap tiny boxes for your tree. Be sure to add a photo of the birthday person at the top of the tree.

Use the tree over and over to celebrate holidays and seasons or for no special occasion at all. How about a Lollipop Tree? You can hang candy coins and play money from the tree to make a Money Tree.

Have children cut out pumpkin shapes to make a Halloween Tree. Hang paper turkeys on a Thanksgiving Tree, paper snowflakes on a Winter Tree, paper hearts on a Valentine Tree, and paper shamrocks on a St. Patrick's Day Tree.

Let children use their imaginations to decorate the trees. Change the decorations every two weeks or so for variety.

Yarn for Birds' Nests

Let children cut short pieces of colored yarn with blunt scissors. It helps if someone holds the yarn ends tight while children cut. In the spring, children can put the yarn outside in the grass for birds to use to build their nests.

Simon Says

You will need:

Scrap paper

Blunt scissors

Play a "Simon Says" cutting game. Give children instructions for which direction to cut. Have children listen and follow the directions.

For example, you could tell children: "Simon says to cut in a straight line. Simon says to turn a corner and cut another straight line. Simon says to turn again and cut another straight line. Simon says to turn a corner and cut one more straight line."

What did they cut? A square or rectangle, maybe.

Let Simon give directions for cutting circles, triangles, zig-zags, and other shapes. If children know left and right, use those directions. If not, use up and down, and point to demonstrate when you say left or right.

Stories on the Road

I am a back-seat rider
Strapped into my seat,
With all the belts and buckles,
The floor won't touch my feet.

There isn't much to do.
No place to run or walk.
I'm really very bored,
And no one wants to talk.

But I felt a tingly thrill
When my older sister said,
"Do you want to hear a story?
It's a special one we've read."

Which story did she choose?
I hope the one today
Will start the way good stories do:
"Long ago and far away . . ."

The words which tell the story
Never seem to last.
"They lived happily ever after . . ."
The ending comes too fast!

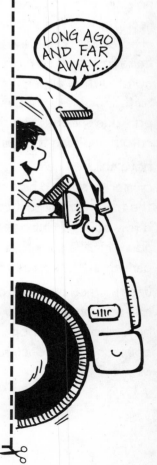

Cut along dashed line and glue to a brown paper lunch bag.

Fun Ideas to Share with Children

I Spy

Choose an object inside the car. Give children a clue, like, "I spy something that is red and fuzzy." Have them ask questions you can answer with "yes" or "no." After someone guesses correctly, let that person choose an object, give a hint, and answer "yes" or "no" questions.

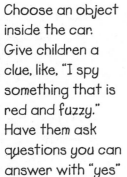

On the outside of this bag you will find the poem *Stories on the Road*. Read the poem aloud with children.

Children easily get bored on car trips, even short ones. Telling stories to each other is a good way to make the time go more quickly.

The Sign Game

As you drive, have children look for letters on signs and buildings along the road. Have them start with the letter A and find each one through to Z.

Pack a Traveling Bag

Advertising Signs Can Start a Story

As you are driving, watch for interesting signs and billboards. Use the names of places advertised or a picture on a billboard as the beginning of a story. Perhaps your story could begin: *What do you think would happen if we turned left at the next exit and stopped at the ostrich farm?* From there you can go on and make up a story with the children about a visit to an ostrich farm.

If you're planning a long car trip, a traveling bag is a must. Even for short trips around town, a traveling bag can prevent young children from getting bored and restless. Use a cloth bag, small plastic basket, shoe box, or any type of container available.

Let children help select items for the traveling bag, like favorite books, crayons, blank paper, a small clipboard, a tape recorder with headphones, story and music tapes, an old catalog, blunt scissors, a stuffed animal or action figure, and small magnetic game boards. If you travel frequently, be sure to change the contents of the traveling bag often.

Number Games

Help children find the numbers from one to ten or one to twenty in order on license plates while you drive.

Once you have found all the numbers in order, play "Find Your Favorite Number." To play you will need paper and pencil. Have each player select a number from one to nine. Each time a person spots their number on a license plate or sign, they get one point. Play to 25, 50, or 100 points.

Tape a Journal

On long trips, let children tape-record the events of your trip. Bring along blank tapes, a tape recorder, and extra batteries. Encourage children to tape at regular intervals or when they see or do something particularly interesting. After one side of the tape is finished, listen to it together.

Color Hunt

Give children paper and a box of 16 crayons. Have them draw a circle with each crayon on the paper. While you travel, have children look for each color. As they find a color, they can cross it off their list.

How Many Red Cars?

Give children paper and a red, green, and blue crayon or marker. Have them draw a large circle with each color. Each time they see a red car, have them make a mark in the red circle. They can make a mark in the green circle for each green car they see, and a mark in the blue circle for each blue car. When the game ends, help children count the marks in each circle. Which circle has the most?

Back-Seat Bingo

Draw pictures of five items for children to look for while you ride, like a dog, fence, green truck, school bus, and bicycle. (If you are the driver, prepare several sets of items on separate sheets of paper ahead of time.)

As children find the items, they can cross them off the list. The first one to find all five calls out, "Bingo!"

Memory Game

Select a category, like animals, fish, birds, or places. The first person says, "one," and names something from the category, like "one dog." The next person repeats, "one dog," and then says, "two," and names something else from the category. Continue repeating the previously named objects in order, and adding one more item each time. See how far you and the children can get before forgetting one. Help each other out with reminders if necessary.

What to Draw

Let children follow your directions to make drawings. They will need paper and pencils. Have an object in mind (a flower, snowman, starfish, bunny, sailboat, and so on) before you begin giving directions. Do not watch while children draw. When they finish, see if what they drew looks like what you had in mind.

String

I found a piece of string

Lying curly on the lawn.

I picked it up and pulled it straight.

It was long, and white, and strong.

I wove it through my fingers,

Laced the string holes in my shoe.

I hopped my way to our garage

To find more "stringy" things to do.

There were buttons near the laundry room,

And, washers, spools, and rings,

Beads and nuts, and pop tops,

And lots of holey things!

So I slipped them on the string

To make a necklace for my friend.

But when I picked the necklace up

They all fell off the end!

Cut along dashed line and glue to a brown paper lunch bag.

Reproducible

String Ball Catch

You will need:

Ball of string

Old, clean nylon stocking
(If using pantyhose, cut off one leg and use that.)

Scissors

Stuff the ball into the open end of the stocking all the way to the toe. Tie off the toe part where the ball is by tying a knot with the remaining part of the stocking. Leave about 10 inches (25 cm) of stocking after you tie it off. Cut off excess. The 10-inch (25-cm) end will give children a "handle" to help catch the ball and toss it back. Playing catch helps young children develop motor skills and coordination.

Spider Webs

Let children "spin a spider web" with a ball of string. They can connect pieces of furniture to each other and weave the string between the objects. Have them select large, heavy objects like beds and chairs to attach the string to and wind it around. After they finish, praise their unique webs. Then have them follow the web backwards and re-roll the string into a ball.

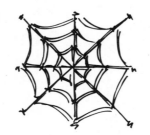

Fun Ideas to Share with Children

On the outside of this bag you will find the poem *String*. Read the poem aloud with children.

String is useful for so many games and activities, from painting to measuring. It gives children an opportunity to practice tying knots and bows, and lets them connect toy cars and trucks together to make a train.

String Weaving

You will need:

Plastic basket (like the ones in which strawberries are sold)

Many pieces of colored string, yarn, and ribbon cut into various lengths

Have children weave a design with the string or yarn through the holes in the berry basket. Line the basket with a paper napkin and fill it with a treat to give to a friend or relative.

String Rhymes

Many words rhyme with *string*. Help children think of words that rhyme. Encourage them to use two and three-syllable words, like *anything*, *something*, and *everything*.

Make up short poems or sentences using words that rhyme with *string*.

Examples: *If you bring me a ring, I'll sing about spring.*

I'd give anything for a nifty ball of string.

Edible Necklaces
You will need:
> A clean, new shoestring
> Cereal with holes (like Cheerios™)

Tie a large knot in one end of the shoestring. The knot needs to be large enough so the cereal won't slip off.

Let children make necklaces by inserting the tip of the shoestring through the holes in cereal. When the shoestring is nearly full, tie the two ends together. Children will enjoy wearing and munching on their edible necklaces or hanging them from trees for the birds to enjoy.

String Gluing
You will need:
> Water-soluble glue
> Waxed paper
> 24" (60-cm) piece of string
> Small, plastic container

Cover the work area with newspaper. Pour glue into the container. Let children place the string in the glue. Coat it well with glue. Place the moist string in a random design on waxed paper. Make sure parts of the string overlap. Press the string together at the overlapping points so it will stick together. When string is dry, have children gently lift it from the paper. The design that results typically looks like lace. Children can use their lacy string designs to decorate a gift package for a friend or family member.

Cat's Cradle
Children enjoy the unique designs that result from different stages of the game "Cat's Cradle." If you don't remember how to play this string game, ask an older child, friend, or relative to help you.

Paint with String
You will need:
> Pieces of string, different lengths
> Washable paints
> Flat tray
> White paper
> Newspaper

Cover work area with newspaper. Be sure children wear old "paint clothes" for this activity. Fold each sheet of paper in half and then unfold it. Pour a thin layer of paint in the tray. Have children dip string into the paint, holding on to one end and saturating the rest of the string.

Have children place the wet string on one half of the paper. Fold the paper over the string at the crease. Gently pull the string from the folded paper. As you pull, press the paper gently with the palm of your hand. Open the paper and look at the wiggly snake-like images.

Let children use another piece of string in the same way on the same paper with a different color paint, or start a new design on another sheet.

Measuring with String

You will need:

    Ball of string
    Blunt scissors
    Objects to measure
    Ruler
    Tape measure

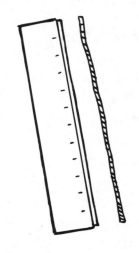

Let children measure objects using the ball of string. Have them cut the string to the length measured. This can also be done to measure the length of a room or the distance between one room and another.

After collecting many string lengths representing measurements taken, show children how to measure each string using a ruler or tape measure.

What Does It Match?

You will need:

    Ball of string
    Scissors
    Objects to measure

When children are not around, measure several objects in a room with string and cut the string to the size of the object. Then invite children to play "What Does It Match?"

Give children premeasured lengths of string. Ask them to use the string to find the object in the room that matches the measurement.

Put Strings in Order

Use the cut strings from "Measuring with String" and "What Does It Match?" activities. Have children put the strings in order by length. Start with the longest and work to the smallest.

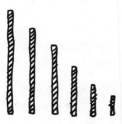

What Good Is String?

Ask children to tell you all the things they can think of for which string can be used. Brainstorm with them after they run out of ideas to encourage them to think of more nonconventional uses for string. Write a list of all the uses suggested. Talk about each idea. Which idea for using string is the best? Which idea is the most creative or unusual?

Have children draw a picture of themselves using string in some way.

Tying Shoes

My fingers don't know how

To weave shoestrings about.

There must be some magic

To make a bow come out.

Everyone has shown me how

The tricky strings should go.

In a week or two I'll learn to tie,

But for now I'll use Velcro.™

Cut along dashed line and glue to a brown paper lunch bag.

Fun Ideas to Share with Children
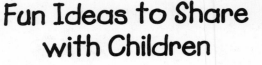

Compare How They Close

Reread the poem "Tying Shoes" out loud to children. Give them adult shoes with shoestrings and ones with Velcro™. Let them explore tying shoestrings and using Velcro™ fasteners. Encourage children to practice tying the adult shoe. It is often easier for children to practice tying larger shoes that are not on their own feet.

Shoe Sort

Put lots of shoes and slippers from all members of the family in a big pile. Have children sort them in various ways: sort to make pairs, sort by color, and sort into two groups—adult and children.

Have children put shoes in order by size. Let them try on other people's shoe and walk around. They can pretend they are the person whose shoes they are wearing.

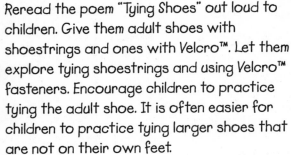

On the outside of this bag you will find the poem *Tying Shoes*. Read the poem aloud with children.

Once children learn to tie knots and bows, they will tie together all the loose ends in your home. Until then, help children practice tying shoes. To master a skill, children must do it over and over again. Provide many fun opportunities for practice!

Tying Shoes
You will need:
  2 different-colored shoelaces
  Old shoe

Insert shoelaces through the bottom eyes of the shoe and tie them together in the middle. Lace up the shoe using the two different-colored laces. The different colors will show the criss-cross pattern of the lacing and make it easier for children to follow the steps when you demonstrate how to tie a shoe.

As you demonstrate, speak out loud, explaining what you are doing in each step: "First I cross the blue lace over the red one. Then I . . . ."

When demonstrating shoe-tying, sit behind children so you are facing the same way they are. This allows them to watch the movements as they would make them, rather than backwards. Encourage children to keep practicing tying the two-tone shoelace on the old shoe.

Measuring Feet

Take children to a shoe store to have their feet measured. Measure both feet. Are they the same size? (It is not unusual for one foot to be a half or full size different than the other.) Have both your feet measured too.

Talk about the instrument used to measure feet. Explain that the number indicates the shoe size and the letter indicates the width. These numbers and letters only have meaning for shoes. They do not have anything to do with age or with the length of feet, even though it looks a bit like a ruler.

At home, trace childrens' feet on a sheet of paper. Write the number and letter of their shoe size. Have them trace your feet too.

No *S* at the End

Most English words add an *s* on the end to show there are more than one of that item. There are several exceptions, and children often find this confusing. (So do some adults.) Explain that the word *singular* means one and *plural* means more than one.

Talk about "funny" words, like *foot* and *feet*, *tooth* and *teeth*, *child* and *children*, *leaf* and *leaves*, *knife* and *knives*, *person* and *people*. Say the singular forms of words and have children say the plurals. Mix up words that use an *s* and those that don't.

Tennis-Shoe Printing with Paint

You will need:
    Old tennis shoes in different sizes
    Washable paint
    Newspaper
    Shallow tray

Cover a table or other large area with newspaper. Pour paint into the shallow tray. Have children dip the bottom of each shoe in paint and make shoe prints on the newspaper. Children can make lots of shoe prints "walking around" on the newspaper.

Measure with Footprints (Non-standard Measurement)

You will need:
    Pencil
    12 sheets of white paper
    Blunt scissors

Trace childrens' feet on paper. Make 12 copies. Let children follow the lines to cut paper footprints. Let children use their paper feet to measure the distance between things in your house.

How many "feet" is the TV from the lamp?

How many "feet" is it from the bedroom to the bathroom?

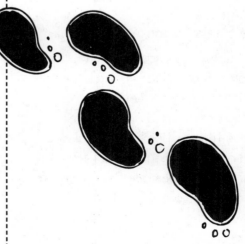

Foot Books

You will need:

Construction paper
Pencil
Scissors
Stapler
Paper feet (from "Measure with Footprints"
activity)

Cut two more same-size "feet" from construction paper for the front and back covers of a book. Use the leftover paper feet from the "Measure with Footprints" activity or make more. Staple the paper feet between the covers.

Let children use the books to write stories about where they walked, jumped, and played during the day. Read the stories at bedtime.

Children often use invented spelling at this age. It is more important for them to know they are successful writers than it is for them to spell words correctly at this point.

Walk in Someone Else's Shoes

Let children walk in different kinds of adult footwear: high heels, sandals, loafers, ballet shoes, slippers, boots, and tennis shoes. Let them try walking outside in golf shoes and baseball or football cleats. Have them notice how the cleats stick in the ground and how they must lift their feet to walk. Talk about which shoes are the easiest to walk in and which are the most difficult.

Shoe Lace Around

You will need:

Heavy construction paper or posterboard
Scissors
72" (180-cm) shoelace
Hole punch

Cut a large shoe or boot shape from heavy construction paper or posterboard. Punch holes one inch (2.5 cm) apart around the edge of the shoe shape. Have children lace around the edge, going in and out of the holes with the shoelace.

Follow the Footprints

You will need:

White paper or brown paper bags
Lightweight cardboard or posterboard
Scissors
Black marker

Trace around a child's shoe on lightweight cardboard or posterboard to make a footprint pattern. Cut lots of footprint shapes from white paper or brown paper bags. On one side, write the numbers from 1 to 20 with a black marker, one number per footprint. On the other side, use a black marker to write the letters from A to Z.

Use the footprints for lots of learning activities. You can use these ideas and make up more of your own:

Let children make a number (or alphabet) trail by putting the footprints in numerical (or alphabetical) order.

Make a trail and let children follow it to find a surprise.

Make one set of footprints with capital letters and another with lowercase letters. Let children match the letter pairs.

The Beach

I like the beach.

Sand is on the beach
So I can build things.

Waves roll on the beach
So I can build wet things.

I can build wet things
Bigger than dry things.

And the things can have corners
If you use both hands,

And round tops too,
If you use a bowl.

Wet things can have
Holes and tunnels,

And I can stick shells on them,
And they'll stay.

I like having water at the beach.
If not, it would be like the sandbox
In my backyard.

And you almost never get
To have water in your sandbox.

I like the beach.

Cut along dashed line and glue to a brown paper lunch bag.

Reproducible

Fun Ideas to Share with Children

Measure, Pour, Sift, and Strain Dry Sand

Fill a dishpan half full of dry sand. Give children sifters, sieves, strainers, measuring spoons and cups, bowls, scoops, and funnels. Have them measure, pour, sift, and strain the sand.

A Note About Sand Activities

Activities that use sand are best done outside because sand can be messy and difficult to clean from carpeting and furniture. You can purchase a large bag of play sand at a very small cost at a building supply store. These activities can easily be done in a sandbox if you have one, or at the beach where sand is plentiful.

Sand Shaker

You will need:

> Empty parmesan cheese shaker or other type of shaker
>
> Sand

Fill the shaker with sand. Have children make mud pies outside, then shake a little sand, like sugar, over the pies. Have them compare the texture of the tops of the mud pies with and without the sand. Save the shaker for other sand activities.

Up Close and Personal

If possible, take children to the beach. Let them play in the sand, build castles from wet sand, search for seashells, and hunt for hidden treasures in the sand.

On the outside of this bag you will find the poem *The Beach*. Read the poem aloud with children.

This type of poem is called *free verse*. The words at the ends of the lines do not rhyme. The lines of the poem are different lengths. After you read this poem to children, ask them what they think about a poem that does not rhyme.

My Free Verse Poem

Let children write a free verse poem about a place they like and tell why they like it. Have them model it after the poem *The Beach*. Help them write the words to their poems on paper and draw accompanying illustrations.

Sand Art

You will need:

> Sand
>
> Glue
>
> Cardboard
>
> Plastic container that holds approximately one cup

Have children draw designs with glue, pouring directly from the bottle onto the cardboard. Give each child one cup of sand to pour over the glue design. Let glue dry about 10 to 15 minutes, then shake off the excess sand.

Treasure Hunt

You will need:
  Dishpan or small pail
  Sand
  Various small objects (like a button, coin, paper clip, rubber band, straw, screw, nut, and washer)

Fill a dishpan or pail half to three-quarters full of sand. Place several small objects in the sand, below the surface so they can't be seen. (Or hide them in your sandbox.) Have children hunt through the sand with their hands for the hidden objects.

When they find an object, have them guess what it is by feel alone. After they guess, they can pull the object out of the sand to check if they were correct.

Constructions with Wet Sand

You will need:
  Dishpan
  Sand
  Water
  Objects that can be used as molds (like butter tubs, cookie cutters, clean half-pint milk containers with the tops cut off, gelatin or candy molds)

Fill a dishpan half full of sand. Add water until the sand is moist and the sand grains stick together. (The sand is moist enough if it retains a print of your hand.)

Let children use molds and their hands to create wonderful structures and shapes from the wet sand. Will they make a magic castle? a sand monster? a throne for a mermaid? You never know what will emerge from a bucket of wet sand.

When the sand dries out, it can be used again for other activities.

Make Your Own Sandpaper

You will need:
  Glue
  Small container
  Small brush
  Bowl of sand
  Craft stick
  Sandpaper
  Water
  Old magazine cover (It is heavier paper and works better than construction paper.)

Let children pour glue into the small container and add one tablespoon of water to thin the glue. Stir with a craft stick.

Have children use the brush to paint glue over the entire surface of the magazine cover. After it is well covered with glue, pour the bowl of sand over the surface, making certain all of the surface is covered. Have them press hard with their hands over the sanded surface.

Let it dry overnight. Shake off the excess sand and they will have a sheet of homemade sandpaper!

Let children compare their sandpaper to the type purchased at a store. They can try sanding a soft pine board with their paper and with store-bought paper to compare the two.

Sand People

You will need:
  Construction paper
  Sand shaker
  Glue

Have children use glue to "draw" a person shape complete with eyes, nose, mouth, ears, and hair. They can add dots of glue for buttons on clothing or jewelry. While the glue is wet, have them shake sand over the paper, covering all the glue areas.

When the glue dries, shake off the excess sand and they will have Mr. or Mrs. Sandman.

Penny in the Sand Bottle

You will need:

    Empty plastic soda bottle with cap

    Sand

    Seashells, small stones, leaves, small twigs, and
        other small natural objects

    Shiny new penny

    Tape or glue

Fill an empty plastic soda bottle three-quarters full of sand. Have children add small seashells, pieces of leaves and twigs, a few small rocks, other natural objects, and one shiny new penny. Seal the top with glue or tape.

Shake up the bottle to hide the penny. Challenge children to find the penny without opening the bottle.

Sand Writing

You will need:

    Dishpan

    Bright-colored construction paper

Place a sheet of bright-colored construction paper in the bottom of a dishpan. Pour a layer of sand about 1/4" (6-mm) deep over the paper. Encourage children to draw and write in the sand using their fingers or a craft stick. The bright paper beneath will reveal what they draw or write as children move their fingers through the sand layer.

This is an excellent way for children to practice making letters and numbers because it offers an opportunity for them to see the letters and numbers with their eyes and feel them with their fingers.

Sand-Print Casts

You will need:

    Sand

    Water

    Plaster of Paris

    Dishpan

    Ruler

    Washable paints and paintbrushes (optional)

Fill a dishpan one-quarter full of sand. Add water until the sand is moist and the sand grains stick together. (The sand is moist enough if it retains a print of your hand.) Press the sand down firmly to compact it.

Smooth the top of the sand with the edge of a ruler. Have children press their hands or feet into the sand about one inch (2.5 cm) deep. Have them carefully remove their hands or feet, leaving impressions in the sand.

Mix plaster of Paris according to the directions on the box. Pour the mixture into the impression. It will take several days for the impression to dry into a cast. Set the dishpan where it will not be disturbed while the plaster dries.

When the cast has completely dried, carefully remove it and brush off the excess sand. If children want, they can paint the cast with washable paint.

Learn More About Animals That Live at the Beach

Take children to the library to find books about animals and plants that live on beaches. *Starfish, Seashells, and Crabs* by George Fichter contains many colorful illustrations of animals children might find at the beach.

Water

Not only is water a liquid to drink,

It's a toy for children to play with, I think.

Children love puddles of rainy water,

Romping and stomping, like a playful otter.

At the drop of a flipper, they'll jump in a pool,

To frolic and splash, or just to stay cool.

They flap their umbrellas in
pouring-down rain,

And watch water gurgle down
the kitchen-sink drain.

They tease their friends with a pointed hose.

They spray it, squirt it, and soak their clothes.

If water is all of those wonderful toys,

Why is it, at bath time, kids
make so much noise?

Cut along dashed line and glue to a brown paper lunch bag.

Umbrella Walk

Take an umbrella walk with children on a warm, rainy day. (No thunder and lighting!) Encourage children to use their senses to learn more about rain.

Look at the rain. How do the raindrops look when they fall? How do they look when they land? Do they splash on concrete differently than they do on grass? Does the rain make objects change colors? Wet rocks often look more shiny than dry ones. Other objects seem to be less colorful. Point out these observations as you walk.

Listen to the rain. How does the rain sound when it hits the umbrella? Does it make a different sound when it hits the sidewalk or the grass? What else sounds like raindrops falling? Does the rain have a rhythm like a song?

Smell the rain. Does the air smell different on a rainy day? Does the grass smell fresher? Ask children why they think rain makes things smell differently.

Taste the rain. Does rain taste like water from the tap? Taste a few drops and find out.

Feel the rain. If it is a warm, gentle rain, children may prefer not to use umbrellas. How is the rain on their skin like taking a shower?

On the outside of this bag you will find the poem *Water*. Read the poem aloud with children.

Children love to play in water. Fill a dishpan or pail with warm, soapy water. Give children scoops, measuring cups and spoons, basters, medicine droppers, funnels, plastic containers, ladles, and other pouring and measuring tools to use for water play.

The Water Sock

You will need:

    2 empty glass jars, about quart-size
    Old white tube sock
    Blue food coloring
    Black marker

Fill one jar half full of water. Add a few drops of blue food coloring. Make a mark on the outside of the jar with a black marker to show the water level.

Place the jar with blue water next to the empty jar. Drape the ends of a sock into the jars, so that at least a quarter of the sock is in each jar. An equal amount of sock should be in both jars.

Tell children they will be conducting an experiment. Ask them to predict what they think will happen to the sock, the blue water, and the empty jar.

Have children check the jars the next day. Some of the blue water will now be in the empty jar. Encourage children to brainstorm ideas to explain how the blue water traveled from one jar to the other.

Keep this science experiment going for three or four days. Let children examine the results every day and observe what changes have taken place.

Raindrop Race

You will need:

Smooth surface, like a piece of Plexiglass™
(A piece of cardboard covered with waxed
paper taped or stapled tightly in place will
also work.)
2 eyedroppers
2 small jars or plastic containers
Water
Blue and yellow food coloring
Dishpan

Fill the containers half full of water. Add a drop or two of blue food coloring to one container and an equal amount of yellow to the other. Place the Plexiglass™ in an empty dishpan so it inclines.

Have children use the droppers to suck blue or yellow water out of the containers and release it drop by drop on the Plexiglass™. Use one dropper only for blue and one only for yellow.

Watch the drops race down the Plexiglass™ into the pan. Have children guess which color will win the race. What happens to the color of the water in the dishpan when the blue and yellow water mix? What happens if more drops of blue are used? What happens if more yellow is used?

Note: Food coloring can be difficult to remove from clothing and other surfaces. Be sure children wear old "paint clothes" and work areas are covered whenever food coloring is used in an activity.

What Good Is Rain?

Talk with children about what rain does for people, plants, and animals. How does rain help people? (Rain helps plants, trees, and crops grow. People need water to drink, for bathing, for washing clothes, for cooking, and so on.)

How does rain help animals? (Animals need water to drink. Many animals live in ponds, lakes, and streams. Frog eggs need water to hatch into tadpoles.)

How does rain help plants? What would happen to plants if they didn't get any water?

Water Painting

You will need:

Small pail of water
Paintbrush
Objects to "paint"

Let children paint different objects with water, like stones, concrete, colored construction paper, cardboard, plastic, and wood. Observe how the items change when wet. Some objects, like colored construction paper and cardboard, will turn a darker color because they absorb water. Some objects do not absorb water, but appear shinier when wet, like stones and plastic.

The Water Cycle

Water falls in the form of rain or snow. When it is cold enough, water freezes to form ice. When the sun warms ice, it turns back into a liquid. The sun causes water to evaporate by changing it to vapor. Water vapor forms clouds which release the water back to the earth in the form of rain or snow.

Have children collect rain water in a plastic container with a wide top. Put the container in the freezer until it becomes solid ice. Talk about how liquid rain water becomes ice naturally. (If it is cold enough, water in lakes, rivers, and ponds freezes and becomes ice.)

Have children put the frozen container of rain water outside in the sunshine and observe what happens. Talk about how the sun melts ice and changes it back to water.

Mark the water level on the container with a black marker. Let the container of melted water remain outside for a few days when no rain is expected. Have children check the water level daily and compare it to the mark made on the container. Talk about where the water went. Point out that clouds contain water vapor, and from clouds, we get rain or snow.

Colored-Water Spray Art

You will need:
   Empty spray bottles
   Water
   Food coloring
   Long sheets of paper

Add water and a few drops of food coloring to the spray bottles to make colored water. Place a long sheet of paper on the sidewalk or lawn. Let children use the spray bottles to make designs with the colored water on the paper. Let them experiment with spraying on the paper from a few inches (or centimeters) away and from farther away to make different patterns. Have lots of paper available since children will want to spray many different designs.

Make a Terrarium

Find a 3-liter soda bottle with a plastic, banded bottom. Get some soil from your yard (or buy potting soil), a scoop, some small plants, and a spray bottle. Use a hair dryer to heat the bottom of the soda bottle and pull off the bottom. Cut off the top of the bottle about a quarter of the way down. Throw away the spout (or cover the large end of the spout with tape and use it for a funnel in the bathtub). Put the dirt or potting soil in the bottom of the soda bottle and plant the plants. Spray them well with water. Place the remaining upper part of the bottle over the plants in the bottom. The "dome" over the plants collects moisture on the inside surface. That accumulated water provides "rain" for the plants.

Tabletop Blocks

Stack the blocks
Up so high,
Tall enough
To touch the sky.

Build a castle,
Then a town.
Make buildings strong
So they won't fall down.

Build a barn
With bright red sides,
And curvy roads
For tractor rides.

Build a city
With signs that show
When to stop
And when to go.

Stack the blocks
On the tray
When it's time
To put them away.

Cut along dashed line and glue to a brown paper lunch bag.

Reproducible

Fun Ideas to Share with Children

Box Blocks

You will need:

> Variety of boxes in different shapes and sizes (like the ones used to package shoes, soap, cereal, crackers, and macaroni)
>
> Brown grocery bags and/or other types of paper
>
> Scissors
>
> Tape
>
> Stickers (optional)

Cut brown grocery bags to size and use them to cover boxes. Tape paper securely in place. For variety, use other types of paper available: left-over wallpaper, construction paper, newspaper, plain white paper, or even gift wrap.

If stickers are available, let children decorate the box blocks with them. The variety of sizes and shapes gives children a great assortment of box blocks to use for their building projects. Because they are larger than ordinary blocks, children can make large constructions in a short time.

Store the boxes in a large plastic bag when not in use. Continue saving empty boxes to add to the box block collection.

On the outside of this bag you will find the poem *Tabletop Blocks*. Read the poem aloud with children.

With a little imagination and a box of blocks, children can create castles, towers, bridges, fences, roads, skyscrapers, and much more.

Building with blocks improves eye-hand coordination and allows children to stretch their imaginations as they progress from building simple towers to more complex structures. Wooden and plastic blocks can be purchased at toy stores, or you can make your own.

Wooden Blocks

You will need:

> 1" x 4" (2.5 cm x 10 cm), 2" x 4" (5 cm x 10 cm), 2" x 2" (5 cm x 5 cm), and 2" x 6" (5 cm x 15 cm) wood scraps (These can usually be obtained free from a job site or at a lumberyard if you ask.)
>
> Saw
>
> Sandpaper
>
> Latex paints and paintbrushes (optional)

Have an adult cut the wood scraps into varying lengths with a saw. Sand the edges to remove rough spots and potential splinters. You and the children can paint the blocks a variety of colors with washable paints.

When the blocks are dry, children can use their imaginations to build towers, castles, and miniature towns.

To keep clutter to a minimum, store blocks in a box with a lid. Children can use the lid as a flat base when building.

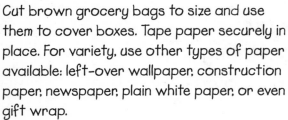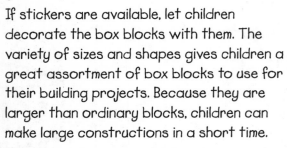

Block Signs

    Crayons or markers
    Magazines and ads
    Scissors
    Glue or glue stick
    Cardboard
    Sticky notes or small pieces of paper and tape

Talk with children about signs they see on stores and buildings. How do signs help you know what is inside buildings? What about the numbers on the fronts of houses and other buildings?

Help children make signs for their buildings on sticky notes or small pieces of paper to attach to wood-block structures with tape. If using box blocks (from the "Box Blocks" activity), they could  write their signs and house numbers directly on the buildings.

Children can cut store logos from ads, glue them to cardboard, and tape them on their block structures.

Let's Compare

Give each child the same number of blocks with similar sizes and shapes. Ask each child to build something with their blocks without looking at the buildings others are making. When they finish, have them compare what they built. Which one is tallest? Were all the blocks used? How are the buildings alike? How are they different?

Talk about how people can create different-shaped buildings with blocks. Try this several times to see how many variations children can build with the same blocks.

Block Math

When children aren't building with blocks, use the blocks for math and counting activities. Line them up in a row. Count the number of blocks together.

Put blocks into two or three small piles. Count the number in each pile. Combine the piles. How many blocks are there altogether?

Put five or six blocks in a pile. Count the blocks with the children. Then take some blocks from the pile. How many are left?

Put five or six blocks in a pile. Count them with the children. Have children turn away while you take a couple of blocks away. Have them count the number left, then tell you how many you took.

Put two, three, or four blocks together in a pile. Ask children to make more piles containing the same number of blocks.

Make two piles of blocks. Have children count the blocks in each pile. Does the first pile contain more, less, or the same number of blocks as the second pile?

Make up story problems together using the blocks:

    If Jo has three blocks and Toni has four blocks, how many blocks do they have in all?

Vary your math and counting activities so children don't get bored. Use these block math ideas as mini-activities that you do for a few minutes at a time, then go on to something else. Many of these math ideas can be applied throughout the day to other objects that you and the children can count, add, subtract, and compare.

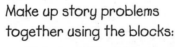

Architectural Designs

You will need:

    Old magazine

    Blunt scissors

    Paper

    Tape or glue

Help children find pictures of the outsides of buildings and other types of structures, like bridges and fences. Have them cut out the pictures and glue or tape them to paper. As  they build with blocks, have them select one of the pictures and try to copy the shape and design. Keep the pictures in a large envelope in the block box for future use. Have children add more pictures when they find appropriate ones.

Introduce Mazes

Most young children have had experience with simple mazes. (For example: *Help the bunny find his way to the carrots.*) If mazes are new to the children, draw a simple maze on paper, explain the word *maze*, and show them how to solve the maze.

Help children build a simple maze with their blocks. Have them run toy cars through the mazes. After doing this together several times, let children build their own mazes for you or others to solve.

How Many Blocks Long?

Help children make a long straight line of blocks. Have them lay down beside the blocks with both feet even with one end. Mark the tops of their heads along the block row. Count the blocks together to find out "how many blocks long" they are.

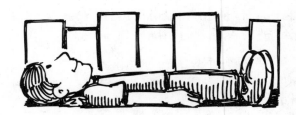

Block Accessories

In addition to wood blocks and box blocks, save other items children can use for building and add these to the blocks box. Small plastic containers from yogurt, single-serving pudding, and applesauce containers, and empty pill bottles can be castle towers and turrets. An empty thread spool or film canister could be a smoke stack on a block train. The more variety in sizes and shapes available, the more children's imaginations will be stimulated.

Note: Be sure to wash all containers thoroughly before allowing children to play with them. Throw out small lids from containers like pill bottles that could present a chocking hazard.

Community Workers

Who brings the mail?

Who walks a beat?

Who puts out fires?

Who cleans our street?

Who checks out books?

Who drives a bus?

Who teaches reading and math to us?

Who cleans our teeth?

Who bakes our pies?

Who takes our trash?

Who checks our eyes?

Who does the work that improves our lives?

Community workers!

Is that a surprise?

Cut along dashed line and glue to a brown paper lunch bag.

Reproducible

Visit Your Local Fire Station

Contact your local fire station and ask for a tour. Usually they welcome parent-child visits and may have special times set aside for tours. As you and the children tour the station they will point out the fire trucks and their accessories, and many pieces of equipment and tools firefighters use. Encourage children to ask questions about what they see.

Seeing a firefighter fully dressed in breathing tanks and air masks at the station can be beneficial to children in the event of a fire. They will be prepared, in advance, for what can be a scary sight in a frightening situation.

Talk about fire prevention and fire safety with children. Discuss your family fire plan. Point out where exits are located and what to do in the event of a fire. Discuss where to meet if they get separated from you during a fire.

Fun Ideas to Share with Children

On the outside of this bag you will find the poem *Community Workers*. Read the poem aloud with children.

Talk with children about the many workers in your community who help us every day.

Write a Letter

You will need:
    Paper
    Pencil
    Envelope
    Stamp

Ask children to write a letter to a family member or friend. Children who cannot write yet can use invented spelling or draw pictures. When the letter is finished, help children fold it and put it in an envelope.

Explain what you are doing as you address the envelope and add your return address. Let children lick the envelopes and apply the stamps. Take a walk with them to the mail box or post office to mail the letter. If you need stamps, let children buy them at the post office.

Talk about what happens to the letter after you mail it and how it gets to the right person.

Here Comes the Fire Truck!

You will need:

- Red paint
- Paintbrush
- Lightweight cardboard
- Foil
- Safety pin
- Tape
- Wire coat hanger
- Scissors
- 4 large paper plates or aluminum foil pie pans
- Child's chair or footstool
- Section of garden hose or other type of plastic hose
- Large cardboard box (Check at an appliance store to see if they have any available.)
- Other items to make the fire truck more realistic

If you can't find a cardboard box large enough for children to sit in, try making one by cutting sides from smaller cardboard boxes and taping them together to make a open large cardboard rectangle.

Help children paint the box red. Put a small chair or footstool inside for the driver's seat. Roll up a piece of plastic hose to attach to the truck with a hook made from a bent wire coat hanger. A broken spray hose and nozzle from a kitchen sink works great too.

Make wheels for the fire truck. Decorate and attach large paper plates or aluminum foil pie pans for the wheels.

Cut firefighter badges from lightweight cardboard and cover them with aluminum foil. Add a star sticker if you have one. Tape a safety pin to the back of the badge so it can be pinned to clothing.

Brainstorm with children about ideas for accessories for the fire truck. How could you make a steering wheel or a ladder for the truck? Could they be cut from scrap pieces of cardboard? Do you have something around the house that would work, like an old bunk-bed ladder?

What could you use to make a bell if you don't have one? What can you use to make hats for the "firefighters"? Do you have any boots firefighters could wear?

When the truck is ready, pretend there is a fire. Call 9-1-1 on a play telephone. Let the firefighters come to the rescue and put out the fire with the hose.

Reproducible

Meet a Police Officer

Call your local police station and ask if a police officer will talk to children for a few minutes about what police officers do. Many police stations have officers who will be glad to talk to children. Allow children to ask questions about what police officers do and the equipment they use. Talk about how police officers can help children.

Community Workers Use Special Vehicles

Use toy vehicles, like garbage trucks, construction equipment, taxis, buses, fire trucks, ambulances, police and sheriff cars, or pictures of these types of vehicles cut from old magazines or newspapers. Talk about what kind of community worker would use each type of vehicle and how they use the vehicles to do their jobs.

Take a Bus Ride

Get a bus-route map. Talk to children about where to go on a bus ride. Mark where you live and where you want to go. Have the amount for the fare ready in advance and let children pay for the bus ride.

As you ride the bus, point out landmarks they know, like a friend's house, a restaurant, school, park, or library they have visited. Help children follow the bus-route map as the bus travels from your home to your destination. This will help children understand better what a map is and how to read it.

Talk about how a bus moves people and their possessions, like packages, school bags, and brief-cases from place to place. Speculate about where different riders on the bus might be going based on what they are carrying and wearing.

Family Mailboxes

You will need:
   Empty, clean, half-gallon milk carton for each family member
   Aluminum foil
   Tape or glue
   Craft sticks
   Red construction paper
   Old purse or cloth bag (optional)
   Old hat for mail carrier (optional)

Cover half-gallon milk cartons with aluminum foil. Secure with tape or glue. Help children make flags by gluing or taping red paper squares to craft sticks. Tape or glue the flags to the cartons.

Make individual mailboxes for each family member and write their names on the foil. You and the children can write notes or draw pictures for other family members. Children can put their school papers in their parents' mailboxes.

Write *Family Mail* on an old purse or cloth bag to use as a mail pouch. Find an old hat for the "mail carrier" to wear. Designate one child in the family as mail carrier for the day. Set a time for the mail carrier to pick up and deliver mail. No peeking in between!

Garbage Trucks in Action!

Garbage trucks are fascinating vehicles to young children. Take time out when the garbage truck comes by and go outside to watch the process with children. If you ask, the driver might crush the garbage while you watch. When you see a truck emptying a dumpster, stop and watch. Talk with children about what happens to trash and what would happen if no one picked up the trash.

Find Community Workers

As you walk with children, have them look for people working outside. You may find mail carriers; street cleaners; police officers; garbage truck, dump truck, and bus drivers; construction workers; tree trimmers; telephone or water department personnel; and many others. Talk about what type of work the people are doing and how that work benefits the community. What would happen if no one did that job?

As you pass buildings, talk about the types of community workers in the buildings and what jobs they do to help the community. Community workers are important, for without them, our communities would not run smoothly.

Learn More About Community Workers

Visit your local library with the children. Ask the librarian to help you find books showing community workers and how they do their jobs.

When I Grow Up

Ask children what kinds of jobs they would like to do when they grow up. Have them draw pictures of themselves doing those jobs.

Who Am I?

Ask children riddles about a community worker and have children guess the answers.

Examples:

I drive people all around town in my vehicle. Many people can fit inside at once. Who am I?

I drive a special truck with a big round broom. I help keep the streets clean. Who am I?

Have children make up their own riddles and you guess the answers.

Charades

Let children take turns pretending to be community workers by showing the actions workers would do at their jobs. No words or sounds are aloud. The other players must guess the type of community worker.

Big Book of Community Workers

Make a book of community workers by stapling several sheets of plain white paper between two pieces of construction paper. Have children cut pictures from magazines and catalogs of people doing different jobs, and glue the pictures to the pages of the book. Children can draw their own pictures of community workers and add them to the book. Under each picture, help children write the name of the job the person is doing and a short sentence about the type of work each one does.

Frog

First comes the egg,
All gooey and sticky.

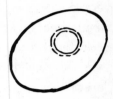

A frog from an egg?
Getting out must be tricky.

Next comes the tadpole,
A strange little creature.

It knows how to swim.
I wonder who's its teacher?

Oh, my goodness!
What do I see?

Legs on the tadpole.
How can that be?

From egg to tadpole,
It doesn't take years.

Two more legs grow,
And the tail disappears.

First egg then tadpole,
And finally a frog

That can hop and croak,
As it sits on a log.

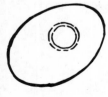

Cut along dashed line and glue to a brown paper lunch bag.

Frog Math

You will need:

    Green and white construction paper
    Black marker
    Scissors

Cut 10 frog shapes from green paper. Put one spot on the back of one frog with a black marker. Put two spots on the second frog, three on the third, and so on, up to 10.

Cut 10 small frog eggs from white paper and write the numbers one through ten on them. Have children match the number on each egg to the number of spots on each frog.

If children are ready to read, cut 10 tadpole shapes. Write the number words from one through ten, one number word per tadpole. Have children match the frogs, eggs, and tadpoles with the same numbers.

Frogs in a Row

Use the 10 frog shapes you cut for the last activity. Have children line them up, in order. Talk about the words *first, second, third,* and so on. Ask children to point to the correct frog when you ask for a specific one: "Can you show me the fourth frog? Which frog is third in line?" Continue with questions using the other number words from *first* through *tenth.*

Fun Ideas to Share with Children

On the outside of this bag you will find the poem *Frog.* Read the poem aloud with children.

Ask children to demonstrate how frogs croak and move around. Join the fun and show them how "adult frogs" hop! Make up frog songs using words that rhyme with *frog* while everyone practices frog hopping.

From Egg to Tadpole to Frog

You will need:

    Black, white, and green felt (or construction paper)
    Scissors
    Glue or glue stick
    Posterboard

Make a story board showing the life cycle of a frog. As you explain each stage of the cycle, place the cut felt pieces on a large uncut piece of felt. If you use construction-paper pieces, tape or glue them to posterboard.

Stage 1. The eggs: Cut one-inch (2.5-cm) ovals from white felt or construction paper. Glue 1/4" (6-mm) black dots on the white ovals. This is the first stage of the cycle.

Reproducible

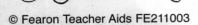

Stage 2. The tadpole hatches: Cut out tadpole shapes from back felt or construction paper. At this stage, the tadpoles have no legs and a long tail.

Stage 3. The tadpole grows: Cut out a black tadpole shape. Add the two legs cut from the same black material.

Stage 4. The tadpole develops: Cut out black tadpole shapes with back and front legs and a shortened tail.

Stage 5. The frog: Cut out a green frog with no tail and four legs.

Use the felt or construction-paper pieces to demonstrate each step in the life cycle of a frog. When you finish, let children use the pieces to repeat the steps in order. If they forget a step or are confused, help them out with hints.

Tadpoles and Their Habitat

Let children watch tadpoles develop into frogs in an aquarium.

What you need:
> 2 to 3 tadpoles (You can purchase these at a pet store or collect them from a local pond or stream.)
> Dirt
> Plastic container
> Rock
> Water

Create a tadpole habitat by putting a five-inch (12.5-cm) layer of dirt in the bottom of an aquarium. Bury all but the top inch (2.5 cm) of a plastic container in the dirt, right-side up. Put an irregular-shaped rock in the bowl. Fill the container partly with water. The top of the rock should remain one to two inches (2.5 cm to 5 cm) above the surface of the water. Allow water to sit 24 hours before adding tadpoles.

Plant small plants in the aquarium, especially around the edges. This provides a hiding place later for the frogs.

The tadpoles will attach to the rock. Let children observe the tadpoles frequently, watching for the appearance of the two front legs, then the two back legs. Notice how the tail gradually disappears.

When the tadpoles become frogs, they will sit on the rock and croak at night (if they are happy frogs!).

If you plan to keep the frogs, cover the aquarium with screening. Buy meal worms at a pet store to feed them. If you release the frogs back to the wild, find a shallow pond. Release the frogs along the margin of the pond in the late afternoon or early evening when the temperature is cooler.

Frog Puzzle
You will need:
- Large color picture of a frog
  (You could photocopy one from a reference book at the library or download one from the Internet.)
- Scissors
- Glue or glue stick
- Posterboard or lightweight cardboard
- Resealable sandwich bag

Glue the frog picture to posterboard and cut it into as many puzzle pieces as children can solve. Make the puzzle difficult enough to offer children some challenge. After children make the puzzle, save the pieces in a resealable bag to use again later.

Save Your Froggy Stories
You will need:
- Green construction paper
- White paper
- Scissors
- Markers
- Stapler
- Magazines and catalogs

Make a large frog-shaped pattern on green construction paper. Cut out two. Use the pattern to cut about a dozen sheets of white paper. Staple the white paper between the green covers.

Let children fill the book with frog drawings, frog stories and poems, and pictures of frogs cut from magazines and catalogs. Ask children to "read" their frog stories to you at bedtime.

More About Frogs and Toads
After you visit the pet store, stop at the library and check out books about toads and frogs. Have children look for ways they are the same and ways they are different. *Turtles, Toads, and Frogs* by George Fichter has many colorful illustrations and interesting frog and toad facts that children will enjoy.

Also check for these books by Arnold Lobel: *Frog and Toad Are Friends, Frog and Toad Together, Frog and Toad All Year,* and *Days with Frog and Toad.*

Visit Frogs and Toads
Go to a pet store where they sell frogs and toads. Ask permission to let the children touch a frog, then a toad. Ask children to describe the difference in the way they feel. Toads are dry and rough. Frogs are wet and smooth.

Lace-up a Frog
You will need:
- Green posterboard
- Scissors
- Hole punch
- 72" (180-cm) shoelace

Cut a large frog shape from green posterboard. Use a hole punch to make holes around the edge of the frog shape, about one-half inch (1.25-cm) apart. Have children use the shoelace to thread through the holes along the edge of the frog. After lacing in one direction, have them lace the posterboard frog back in the other direction.

Painting

I'm picky when I paint,
Because I want to see
The colors brushed on paper
In a way that pleases me.

I love to paint *my* own way
To see what I can do.
It doesn't really have an end, you know,
I just stop when I am through.

I brush the paint upon the page;
I watch it roll and drip.
Sometimes I cover all the spaces,
Sometimes only a little bit.

When all the page is painted
And I set it down to dry,
I feel so warm and wonderful,
But please don't ask me why.

The way I feel when painting,
I can only tell a little.
There's a start, and there's an end,
But the joy is in the middle!

Cut along dashed line and glue to a brown paper lunch bag.

Fun Ideas to Share with Children

Experiment with Paint Applicators

You will need:

    Paintbrushes

    Paint

    Items that can be used to apply paint

Let children use different sizes and types of paintbrushes, like bristle brushes and foam brushes or a paint roller. What other objects can they use to paint?

Each time they want to paint, let them try something different. They can experiment with pot scrubbers, cotton swabs, feathers, roll-on bottles (empty deodorant bottles), chopsticks, straws, cotton balls, twigs, leaves, squeeze bottles, toothbrushes, and sponges.

Each item will give a slightly different texture to paint when it is applied. Use any of these with washable paint found at craft stores or in the school supply section of most stores. Children can suggest other items that might also work to apply paint.

Don't forget the most popular tool children enjoy using to apply paint—their fingers.

On the outside of this bag you will find the poem *Painting*. Read the poem aloud with children.

Why do children love to paint? Is it because they like to see the bright colors appear on paper or because they usually end up with as much paint on themselves as they do on the paper? Find an old adult shirt for children to wear over their clothes when they paint, and let them create masterpieces. Here are several ideas for making different types and textures of paint and for items children can use to apply it.

Experiment with Paper

You will need:

    Paintbrushes

    Paint

    Different types of paper

Different types of paper provide new and interesting surfaces for painting. Let children experiment painting on sandpaper, waxed paper, dinner napkins, cardboard, newspaper, brown paper bags, aluminum foil, corrugated paper, and tissue paper.

Paint will react differently on each surface and provide new experiences for children.

97

Glitter Galore

You will need:

    1/2 cup liquid starch
    1 tablespoon glitter
    Black or dark-blue construction paper
    Paintbrush
    Small container

Mix the liquid starch and glitter in a small plastic container. As children paint, have them stir the glitter paint each time they dip the paintbrush to keep the glitter from settling to the bottom.

After they finish, the starch will dry to a clear, shiny finish. When the solution dries, the glitter is very visible against the dark paper background. This type of paint is great for making holiday greeting cards or painting night scenes with snow falling.

Cool Paint for Winter Scenes and Icy Landscapes

You will need:

    1 cup Epsom salts
    1/2 cup water
    Small container
    Black or dark-blue paper
    Paintbrush

Heat Epsom salts and water in a pan over low heat until the solution is clear. Pour into a small container.

Let children use a paintbrush or any of the experimental paint applicators suggested previously to paint on black paper. When the mixture dries it looks cold, wintery, and icy. It works particularly well for painting winter scenes and icy landscapes.

Leftover paint can be stored in a jar with a lid. The mixture will keep for many months.

Slimy Paint Is Fun!

You will need:

    2 tablespoons corn syrup
    1/2 cup washable paint
    Paintbrush
    Paper

Most children enjoy painting with this thick paint because of the texture. Let children apply this slimy paint with one of the previously suggested paint applicators. Don't be surprised if children's favorite applicators become their fingers for this paint.

Get Down to the Nitty-Gritty Paint

You will need:

    1/2 tablespoon play sand
    1/2 cup paint
    Paintbrush
    Paper

Let children apply this gritty paint with one of the previously suggested paint applicators. The paint will have the texture of sandpaper when it dries. This paint is especially good for painting beach scenes.

Lumpy Paint

You will need:

  2 tablespoons flour
  1/2 cup paint
  Paintbrush (or other paint applicator)
  Paper

Mix the flour and paint. Don't worry about making a smooth mixture, this paint is supposed to be lumpy! When it dries, the paint will crack, which results in an interesting lumpy texture.

This paint is great for pictures of rocky landscapes.

Add Sparkle to Paintings

You will need:

  1/2 cup salt
  1/2 cup paint
  Paintbrush (or other paint applicator)
  Black or dark-blue paper

Mix salt and paint. Let children paint the Milky Way galaxy or the stars at night on dark-blue paper. The paint will be sparkly and bright.

Colors and Lines

You will need:

  4 marbles
  Shallow box
  Paper
  Plastic spoons
  4 colors of paint
  4 small containers

Pour about a half-inch (1.25 cm) of each color paint in a container. Put one marble in each of the four containers of paint.

Have children place a sheet of paper in the shallow box and use the plastic spoon to pick up one of the marbles and drop it onto the paper. Have them roll the marble around in the box by tilting the box. Remove the marble with the spoon. Repeat the process with each color.

What Can I Do?

I'm hiding from you.
What will you do?

If you will find me,
Then I will find you!

I'm running from you.
What will you do?

If you will chase me,
Then I will chase you!

I'm talking to you.
What will you do?

If you listen to me,
Then I will listen to you!

I'm singing to you.
What will you do?

If you dance with me,
Then I'll dance with you!

I'm smiling at you.
What will you do?

If you give me a hug,
I'll give you two!

Cut along dashed line and glue to a brown paper lunch bag.

Fun Ideas to Share with Children

Shadow Dance

You will need at least two people for this activity. You can invite one of your child's friends to participate, but it would also be fun if you are the "shadow." Play some fun music.

One child becomes the leader for each song. The others face the leader who dances or moves in time to the music. Those facing the leader match the movements of the leader, becoming the leader's shadows.

Hide-and-Seek

Play Hide-and-Seek with children. Invite some of the children's friends to play too. The child who is "it" gets practice counting to 10, while the others hide. Most young children enjoy finding small nooks and crannies to hide in, but their giggles usually give them away.

On the outside of this bag you will find the poem *What Can I Do?* Read the poem aloud with children.

Sometimes young children feel overwhelmed because of the number of things they cannot do yet, or cannot do as well as adults. Encourage them to talk about all the wonderful things they can do, like tie a shoe, count to 10, run fast, paint a picture, button and zipper clothing, and so on. Concentrate on the positives. Talking about children's accomplishments helps build their self-esteem.

The "I Can" Book

You will need:

White paper
Construction paper
Stapler
Crayons, markers, or colored pencils

Make an "I Can" book by stapling several sheets of white paper between two sheets of colored construction paper. Let children draw pictures on each  page of the many wonderful things they can do. When they have filled their books with pictures, have them dictate a story about something they can do well. Write out the stories and read them back at bedtime.

When I Grow Up . . .

What you need:

Blunt scissors

Old magazines

Large envelope

Write *When I Grow Up . . .* on the envelope. Let children look through magazines for pictures of people in action (dancing, working at a job, painting, climbing a mountain, driving a plane, and so on). Ask them to cut out pictures of people doing things they want to do when they grow up. Save the pictures in the envelope. Let children add more pictures to the envelope every few months.

Play Charades

Have children take turns acting out the names of stories, books, or movies or scenes from stories or movies without using any words. Have the others guess the name of the story, poem, or movie. Don't forget that you should take a turn too.

Smiling Faces

Give children hand mirrors. Ask them to smile in as many different ways as they can. After they have practiced in the mirror, have them look at their reflections in the bowl of a large metal spoon and smile. Have them smile while looking at the back of the spoon. Do the different reflective surfaces change how their smiles look?

Have children find other surfaces in the house that will reflect a smile (window glass, aluminum foil, glass on a framed picture, the TV screen, someone's sunglasses).

Hugs

Everyone needs lots of hugs. Be generous with your hugs. Give children lots of hugs every day. Ask children how hugs make them feel? What are good times to get hugs? What are good times to give hugs?

If you could see a hug, what would it look like? Ask children to draw a picture of how they think a hug might look.

"I Can" Poem

I can hop and skip.
I can draw a ship.

I can tie my shoe.
I can dance for you.

Read the above sample "I Can" poem to children. Help them make up two lines that rhyme, naming things they can do. Write each pair of lines on a separate sheet of paper. When they finish the poem, read each page back to them and have them add an illustration. Staple the pages together between two pieces of construction paper to make a book. Write a title on the cover using the child's name and one or two action words from the poem (example: "Jessica Can Hop and Skip").

Shadow Tag

On a bright, sunny day, children can play "Shadow Tag." Play this game the same way you play tag, but instead of the person who is "it" tagging another player, the person must tag the other player's shadow.

Reproducible

You and Me

Look in the mirror;
Who do you see?
A reflection of you.
It couldn't be me.

You have blue eyes.
I have brown.
You have an "up nose."
Mine points down.

You use your left hand.
I use my right.
You drink milk.
I like Sprite™.

You eat cake.
I like pie.
You can braid.
I want to tie.

That's what friends
Are all about,
Being different together,
Working things out.

Cut along dashed line and glue to a brown paper lunch bag.

Handprints

You will need:
- Paper
- Washable paints
- Shallow tray
- Wet paper towels
- Newspaper

Cover the work surface with newspaper. Pour about a quarter-inch (6 mm) of paint into a shallow tray. Let children place their hands in the paint, then make handprints on paper. (If you don't mind, children would love to do the same with their bare feet.)

Let other children and adults participate, each making handprints on different pieces of paper. Have children compare the handprints. How are they alike? How are they different?

Use wet paper towels for quick cleanup of hands (and feet) when you finish.

Fun Ideas to Share with Children

On the outside of this bag you will find the poem *You and Me.* Read the poem aloud with children.

Talk with children about how they are alike and different than their friends. Accent the ways they are alike. Talk about how people can be friends even if they seem very different in many ways.

Draw Faces from Mirror Reflections

You will need:
- Hand mirror
- Crayons
- Paper

Have children draw their faces by copying what they see in the mirror.

Talk about how people's faces are alike: everyone has two eyes, one nose, and one mouth. Talk about how people's faces are different: size and shape of eyes, nose, and mouth; eye, hair, and skin color.

Family Resemblances

Collect photographs of many family members at different ages. Talk about how family members often look like each other in some ways. Have children look for characteristics that family members share. Do they have the same-shaped nose as their grandfather? Are their eyes exactly like Aunt Ellen's? Are they as tall as Uncle Josh at the same age?

105

Feel with Your Fingers

Make a blindfold and place it over one child's eyes. Place another child in front of him or her. Have the blindfolded child use fingers to feel the face of the other child and describe the child's features. Let children take turns. Talk about how feeling objects with our fingers can give us information about the world around us.

Draw Shadows

Take children outside on a sunny afternoon. Find a flat place on the sidewalk or driveway where children's shadows show clearly. Trace the outlines of the shadows with sidewalk chalk while children stand still. After tracing, have them lie down on their shadow outlines. Let them compare the difference in the size of the outline and the size of their bodies.

Try this in the same place early in the day and later in the afternoon. Have children notice how the size of their shadows change.

Face Words

Have children name as many "face" words as they can. Write the words on paper. Help them count the words they listed. Encourage them to discover words like *lips, smile, cheek, eyes, lashes, eyebrows, chin, forehead, hair, dimples, skin,* and *nose.*

Face Collage

You will need:
   Blunt scissors
   Glue or glue stick
   Old magazines and catalogs
   Large sheet of paper or posterboard

Have children cut pictures of people's faces from old magazines and catalogs. Help them try to find many different kinds of faces, young and old, smooth and wrinkled, hairy and freckled. Look for pictures of people with different-colored eyes and hair and from different races.

Have children glue the pictures to the posterboard, overlapping some pictures, until the entire surface is covered. Talk about how the faces in the pictures are the same and how they are different.

Foods I Like

Staple several sheets of blank paper between two construction-paper covers. Have children name foods they like to eat. Write the list on the first inside page of the book.

On each succeeding page, have children draw a picture of one food item on their list. Encourage children to write the name of the food below the

drawing. At this age, children often use invented spelling. Don't discourage them or worry about spelling words correctly at this point. It's more important for them to be successful as writers than it is to spell all the words correctly.